Quick Vocabulary Power

Wiley Self-Teaching Guides teach practical skills from accounting to astronomy, management to mathematics. Look for them at your local bookstore.

Math

All the Math You'll Ever Need: A Self Teaching Guide, by Steve Slavin
Geometry and Trigonometry for Calculus, by Peter H. Selby
Practical Algebra: A Self-Teaching Guide, by Peter Selby and Steve Slavin
Quick Algebra Review: A Self-Teaching Guide, by Peter Selby and Steve Slavin
Quick Arithmetic: A Self-Teaching Guide, by Robert A. Carman and Marilyn J. Carman
Quick Business Math: A Self-Teaching Guide, by Steve Slavin
Quick Calculus: A Self-Teaching Guide, by Daniel Kleppner
Statistics: A Self-Teaching Guide, by Donald Koosis

Business Skills

Accounting Essentials: A Self-Teaching Guide, by Neal Margolis and N. Paul Harmon
Making Successful Presentations: A Self-Teaching Guide, by Terry C. Smith
Managing Assertively: A Self-Teaching Guide, by Madelyn Burley-Allen
Managing Behavior on the Job: A Self-Teaching Guide, by Paul L. Brown
Selling on the Phone: A Self-Teaching Guide, by James Porterfield
Successful Time Management: A Self-Teaching Guide, by Jack D. Ferner

Science

Astronomy: A Self-Teaching Guide, by Dinah L. Moche
Basic Physics: A Self-Teaching Guide, by Karl F. Kuhn
Biology: A Self-Teaching Guide, by Steven D. Garber

Languages

Advanced Spanish Grammar: A Self-Teaching Guide, by Marcial Prado
French: A Self-Teaching Guide, by Suzanne A. Hershfield
German: A Self-Teaching Guide, by Heimy Taylor
Italian: A Self-Teaching Guide, by Edoardo A. Lebano
Spanish Grammar: A Self-Teaching Guide, by Marcial Prado

Other Skills

How Grammar Works: A Self-Teaching Guide, by Patricia Osborn
Listening: The Forgotten Skill, A Self-Teaching Guide, by Madelyn Burley-Allen
Quickhand: A Self-Teaching Guide, by Jeremy Grossman
Study Skills: A Student's Guide for Survival, A Self-Teaching Guide, by Robert A. Carman

Quick Vocabulary Power

A Self-Teaching Guide

Jack S. Romine
Henry Ehrlich

John Wiley & Sons, Inc.
New York • Chichester • Brisbane • Toronto • Singapore

Copyright © 1996 by John Wiley & Sons, Inc.

Library of Congress Cataloging-in-Publication Data

Romine, Jack S.
    Quick vocabulary power: a self-teaching guide / Jack S. Romine and Henry Ehrlich.
        p.   cm. — (Wiley self-teaching guides)
    Rev. ed. of: Vocabulary for adults. 1975.
    Includes index.
    ISBN 0-471-05008-3 (acid-free paper)
    1. Vocabulary—Problems, exercises, etc.   I. Ehrlich, Henry,
1949–   . II. Romine, Jack S.   Vocabulary for adults.   III. Title.
IV. Series.
PE1449.R667   1995
428.1—dc20   95-30999

Printed in the United States of America

10 9 8 7 6 5 4 3 2 1

Contents

Introduction

If you picked up this book, your command of vocabulary obviously is not what you would like it to be. *Quick Vocabulary Power* can help. First published in 1975 under the title *Vocabulary for Adults,* it was based on a very interesting premise—namely, that because a great deal of English vocabulary is derived from Greek and Latin roots, greater familiarity with those roots can help you use the English language with greater authority and confidence.

Society has changed since 1975 in ways that affect the way we use English. Some facts of everyday life have changed, and many of the examples in the original edition of this book would have little immediate meaning for contemporary readers, which is a primary reason for publishing a revised text.

One of the biggest changes is the pervasive use of computers and other technology. Any discussion of the Greek prefix *micro,* for example, would be incomplete without some reference to *microchips* or *microwaves,* while *microfilm,* which appeared in an example in the original edition, isn't nearly as important now.

However, the Greek and Latin roots remain what they were in the original edition—building blocks for the way we read, speak, and write English, and thus for the way we think. They are part of the living language in the 1990s for the same reason that they were part of it in 1975, 1776, or 1066.

A computer-expert friend of mine gave me an interesting contemporary insight into why classical languages are important. He was asked by a student which computer languages to study. Instead of answering COBOL or other languages in current use, my friend told the student to learn FORTRAN, which hasn't been used for years. He said, "It's a classical language, and the modern languages come out of it. Not that many computer scientists study the classical languages anymore, and the ones that don't are missing something important." Latin and Greek are to English what FORTRAN is to COBOL.

Jack S. Romine, who wrote the original edition of this book, explained that we all have two vocabularies. One comprises essentially short, mainly Anglo-Saxon words like father, mother, earth, sky, sun, moon, cow, fire, water, go, and pray. These are the words that make up everyday speech, and most of us already use them effectively.

The second vocabulary is more formal and academic. Many of these words, such as *dysfunction, metamorphic, empathy,* and *syllogism,* are derived from the classical languages. This book is concerned mainly with those words.

The academic words are the ones that slow you down when you are reading, or are subject to fine shades of meaning that serve to either clarify or confuse, depending on how well you use them. For example, a person who can't distinguish between an *epithet* and an *epitaph* may insult the dead and crush the living. *Epithet* combines the Greek prefix *epi-* (meaning *on* or *upon*) with the root *thet,* which means *put. Epitaph* combines the same prefix with the root *taph,* which means *tomb.* An *epithet* is an insult, commonly used in the phrase "hurl an epithet." An *epitaph* is a message on a tombstone. Ambrose Bierce defines an epitaph with tongue in cheek as "an inscription on a tomb, showing that virtues acquired by death have a retroactive effect."

If you carve an *epithet* on a tombstone, you will offend the mourners. On the other hand, if you hurl an *epitaph,* the tombstone would do far more damage to the target than a mere insult.

People who confuse words like epitaph and epithet are frequently mocked. These mistakes are called malapropisms, named for a character named Mrs. Malaprop in a 1775 play called "The Rivals" by British playwright Richard Sheridan. Mrs. Malaprop (whose name comes from the French words *mal apropos,* meaning inappropriate) constantly made such mistakes, to the great amusement of audiences ever since. This book can help you avoid malapropisms yourself.

Once you begin to break the hard words down into their components, you will have a shortcut to understanding and using them. For example, the Latin root *cur,* from *currere,* or run. If you swim against the current, you swim "against running" water. A *recurrent* illness keeps "running back," or happening again and again. A day's excursion to a museum is "running outside" whereas an *incursion* of relatives is when they "run into" your house and eat all your food. A sore throat may be the *precursor* of the flu, and a *courier* is someone who runs messages from your office to someone else's.

Sometimes, knowledge of the Greek and Latin will help you decipher useful English words. For example, if a doctor prescribes an unfamiliar treatment like *diathermy,* you will recognize that it comes from the prefix *dia,* which means through, and *therm,* which means heat. Thus, the treatment will consist of "heating your tissue through."

In some cases, the English words remain identical to their Greek and Latin roots, like *thermometer,* which means "that which measures heat." Other words have gained new meaning through use.

Jack Romine pointed out in his original introduction that symposium simply meant "drinking together," but that it has since come to mean a gathering for purposes of exchanging ideas, usually on a single topic. The Greeks probably used the occasion of drinking together as an opportunity to exchange ideas, and the drink fueled the discussion. As Mr. Romine observed, the modern symposium is generally accompanied by a good deal of drinking, but that is not its primary purpose.

In each section of this book, when words are used somewhat differently than their Latin or Greek components would suggest, we make an effort to give these meanings. As a matter of course, if you really want to understand modern English, you must be able to distinguish between *denotation*—what words literally mean—and *connotation*—special meanings that words acquire from use in a living language. The best clues to connotation are a good current dictionary and the context of the word in a sentence.

The final section of this book, on confusables, is new. Confusables are words that are commonly used mistakenly for one another. Most of these are based on the wrong use of the building blocks just described, but others are based on sound, and some just on carelessness or ignorance.

Finally, I would like to say a bit about my own qualifications for revising this interesting book. I am a speechwriter and the author of books and commentary about the craft of speechwriting. The language of speechwriting is really a hybrid of the two kinds of vocabulary that Jack Romine described—the familiar and the academic. Some of the words dealt with in this book are unsuitable for speeches. They are too hard to pronounce, or their similarities to other derivatives of the same roots are grounds for confusion, both to speaker and to audience. Keep in mind that effective expression depends on the vocabulary of the listener or reader as well as that of the speaker or writer. A speechwriter has to be careful not to leave an audience behind through the use of excessively hard words. You may never have to write a speech, but you don't want to leave yourself or your audience behind as you stretch your vocabulary either. Still, the search for the right word is well worth it. Mark Twain wrote, "The difference between the right word and the wrong word is the difference between lightning and lightning bug." This book should make the search for the right word a good deal easier.

—Henry Ehrlich

How to Use This Book

This book's self-teaching format is organized very simply. The first chapter introduces the word parts—root, prefixes, and suffixes—and shows how they combine to form a number of English words. There is then a brief self-test.

Chapters 2 through 6 are divided into units that focus on specific Greek or Latin word parts. Each unit covers one word part that is shown with the other roots, prefixes, and suffixes with which it is commonly used. There are also brief definitions of their meanings. For example:

GEN: birth, race, kind

Prefixes	Other roots	Suffixes
con: with	*cid:* kill	*al:* that which
de: reverse of	*logy:* study of	*al:* being
pro: forward	*photo:* light	*ate:* verb ending
	psych: mind	*ist:* one who
		or: one who
		us: that which
		y: that which

You will note that there are some variations in certain forms. For example, the suffix "y" is defined as "that which," but it is also defined as "act of" and "state of." Another example is "logy," which can mean "discussion of," or "study of" or "words of." A full list is supplied in the appendix.

This is followed by a selection of the derivatives that they combine to form. By referring from the derivatives to their component parts, you will be able to tell how they were formed and what the derivatives mean. (Frequently, you will notice overlap between word part sections, which should help reinforce your understanding.) The derivatives are also presented with simplified pronunciation.

For example:

Derivatives: congenital (kuhn JEN ih tuhl)
degenerate (dee JEN er ate)
gene (JEEN)
genealogy (jee nee AHL uh jee)
generate (JEN er ate)
genitals (JEN ih tuls)
genocide (JEN uh side)
genus (JEE nuss)

In each unit you will then practice new words, sometimes by defining additional words based on the information already given, and in other cases by supplying the words themselves. If the words as commonly used now mean something very different from what their Latin and Greek roots would suggest, this study section will help you understand the current meanings. While practicing, cover the left column with your hand or a piece of paper, then fill in the answers in the right column.

For example:

• **birth, race, or kind**   The chemical units that carry hereditary characteristics from parents to offspring are called *genes*. Genes, then, determine the characteristics of

_____.

• **worse**   If a plant or animal strain *degenerates,* does it become better or worse?

At the end of each unit is a self-test, which is followed by the answers. Do each test to check your progress—if you get more than two or three wrong, go back over the unit to reinforce the new words.

You will notice that many words and word parts—roots, prefixes, and suffixes—are defined differently in different parts of this book. Don't be thrown by the inconsistencies. Words acquire shades of meaning when they are used, and these words have been used for thousands of years. The meanings given for each entry are those that are most precise for use in the particular combination of word parts that combine to form a particular larger word.

For example, the prefix *de* is defined as both down and away. In combination with the root *scribe,* which means write, it makes describe. It's difficult to see the connection between "write away" and describe. But write down is pretty clear—you can write down various characteristics to describe something.

The suffix *-ile,* is defined as "that which" in the word projectile. It is combined with the prefix *pro,* which means forward, and the root *ject,* which means throw. A projectile, therefore, is "that which is thrown forward."

In the word *facile,* however, *ile* is define as able, because it is combined with the root *fac,* meaning "do" or "make." If you describe someone as facile, you are saying they are able to do something rather easily.

Roots and prefixes are compiled in the appendix for easy reference, according to their Greek and Latin origins. Since the suffixes come from many sources, they don't lend themselves to easy categorization by origin. However, they are compiled in a list that gives all their definitions as used in the book.

Don't be thrown either by the fact that sometimes Latin word parts appear in combination with Greek ones. The Romans took much of their culture from the Greeks and the rest of us have borrowed from both ever since. Likewise, don't get sidetracked by slight variations in spellings. These, too, are part of the wear and tear of living language. Pronunciation changes. Letters are added and dropped along with sound.

For simplicity's sake, we have taken liberties with certain words that linguists might protest. The word psycho is an example. It is listed as a root. In fact, the root is psyche, which comes from the name of a mythological character. The word means mind. Psyche is rarely used. We almost always use the combining form psycho, to create words like psychology or psychopath. This is an introductory book, and it would be counterproductive to explain the intricacies of each word.

Chapters 7 and 8 are a little different. Chapter 7 teaches you the Greek and Roman numbers, which are often used as parts of words.

Chapter 8 covers what I call *confusables,* which are words that sound alike and are often mistaken for each other. Here you'll learn how to distinguish these words from each other so that you use each when you really mean it.

At the end of the book, you'll find a Final Vocabulary Power Self-Test. This will wrap up the book and show you how much you've learned. It may be a good idea to retake this test once every few months to be sure that you haven't forgotten your new words. The Appendix defines all the roots and prefixes used in the book. You can refer to this as a quick refresher after you've finished the Vocabulary Power program.

You're about ready to start. As you get ready, keep these tips for effective studying in mind:

- Pronounce all word parts, derivatives, and their English meanings.
- Write down the answer in both the self-teaching section and the self-test.
- Work faster on the material that comes easily and slow down on the harder sections.
- Don't move on till you feel comfortable.
- Begin each session with a brief review of the previous one.

1 Word Parts

This chapter introduces the word part approach that will be used throughout this book. The box is to be used as you read through this first chapter. First, read the information in the box carefully. Then begin reading the right column below, covering up the left column with your hand or a piece of paper. When you come to an answer blank or question, write your answer in the space provided. Whenever it is helpful, look back at the box. Then check the book's answer in the left column, on the same line. If you have answered correctly, continue reading. If not, reread the previous few lines. Often you can see a part that you misread or overlooked. Correct your answer and then go on.

• **root**	According to the panel, every English word contains a word part or basic meaning called a(n) _____.
• **prefix**	A word part placed in front of a root is called a(n) _____. In the word *reshape*, the root is *shape* and the prefix is
• **re**	_____.
• **again** • **again**	The prefix *re* often has the meaning "again." Thus, *reread* means "read _____," and *reshape* means "shape _____."

About Word Parts

Every word in English has a **root** or basic meaning. Often, the root itself forms a complete word, such as *sure* or *shape,* but a root may also be a unit that is not used by itself, such as *dict* (say) in the word *predict.*

A *prefix* is a word part placed in front of a root to change the meaning. Examples are *unsure* (un + sure), *reshape* (re + shape), and *predict* (pre + dict). The prefixes added in the examples change the meaning: *unsure* means "not sure," *reshape* means "shape again," and *predict* means "say before" (that is, "say ahead of time").

More than one prefix can be placed in front of a root:

renew (re + new) = to make new again

nonrenewable (non + re + newable) = not able to be renewed

A *suffix* is a word part placed after a root. It tells us whether a word is being used as a noun, a verb, an adjective, or an adverb. Here are examples:

Nouns: *coolness* (cool + ness), *amusement* (amuse + ment), *diction* (dict + ion)

Verbs: *dictate* (dict + ate), *terrorize* (terror + ize), *walking* (walk + ing)

Adjectives: *joyous* (joy + ous), *useful* (use + ful), *restless* (rest + less)

Adverbs: *quickly* (quick + ly), *tamely* (tame + ly)

More than one suffix can be placed after a root. A word existing as one part of speech can be changed to another by adding an additional suffix.

Adjective: *helpful* (help + ful)

Adverb: *helpfully* (help + ful + ly)

Noun: *helpfulness* (help + ful + ness)

Many different words with different meaning can be formed merely by adding various prefixes and suffixes to a root. These words are called derivatives. Below are just a few of the derivatives of the root *ject,* which means "to throw."

project	projectile	interjection
projected	eject	conjecture
projecting	ejected	conjectural
projection	ejecting	reject
projectionist	ejection	
projector	interject	

Words may also be formed by putting two roots together.

thermometer = thermo (heat) + meter (measure) = that which measures heat

democracy = demo (people) + cracy (rule) = rule by the people

- **arrange again**   What does *rearrange* mean? _____

- **restyle**   If a woman wished to style her hair in a different way, she would _____ it. (put together two word parts that mean "style again")

- **re**
- **clean**
- **clean again**

The word *reclean* divides into the prefix _____ and the root _____ and means "_____."

- **no**

The combination *re* is not a prefix unless it is placed before a root whose meaning it can change. In the word *red*, *re* is not a prefix because there is no root for it to change: (re + d). Neither is it a prefix in the word *rent* (re + nt). Now test the word *ready* to see if it contains the prefix *re*: (re + ady). Do you recognize *ady* as a word you already know? _____ Does it help explain the meaning of

- **no**
- **no**

the larger word *ready*? _____ Is *re*, then, a prefix in *ready*? _____

- **preview**

The prefix *pre* often means "ahead of time." Apply this rule-of-thumb test for a prefix to these three words: *press, preview, preach*. In which word(s) does *pre* occur as a prefix? _____

- **view ahead of time**

The word *preview* means "_____." Not all roots make complete words in themselves. In the box, for example, several words are derived from the root *dict*, meaning "say." Now look at the word *recur*, derived from the root *cur*, meaning "run." When *re* is added to *cur*, the expanded meaning becomes run

- **again**
- **recur**

_____. If an illness is likely to "run (its course) again," we say that it may _____.

- **not certain**

The prefix *un* means "not." When added to the root *certain*, it makes a new word meaning _____.

- **un**

What would you add in front of the root *seen* to give the meaning "not seen"? _____ *Under* and *untrue* both begin with the

- **untrue**
- **not true**
- **happy / un**
- **not happy**

combination *un*, but it is a prefix only in the word _____, meaning "_____." In the word *unhappy* the root is _____, the prefix is _____, and the meaning is "_____."

- **nonrefillable**

More than one prefix can be placed in front of a root. A medicine that can be *refilled* without another prescription is *refillable* (re + fillable)—

literally, able to be filled again. If *non* means "not," form the word that means "not able to be filled again." _____

- non
- re

- more than one

The two prefixes added to *nonrefillable* are _____ and _____. *Nonrefillable* illustrates the principle that (write the correct choice): only one/more than one _____ prefix can be added in front of a root.

- suffix

Now look at the panel. A part added after a root is called a(n) _____. It indicates whether a word is being used as a noun, a verb, an adjective, or an adverb.

- ness

In the word *coolness*, the root is *cool* and the suffix must therefore be _____.

- amuse
- ment

In the word *amusement* the root is _____ and the suffix is _____.

- judge

The suffix *ment* often has the meaning "act of." Thus, *argument* (argue + ment)* means "act of arguing" and would be used as a noun: Her *argument* is logical. In the word *judgment** the root is

- ment
- act of judging

_____, the suffix is _____, and the meaning of the word is "_____." The suffix *ment* indicates that *judgment* is being used as what part of speech?

- a noun

(Check the box if you're not sure.) _____

- ness

Another common suffix is *ness*. If you are very happy, you are in a "state of happi_____." If you dislike things that

- ugliness

are ugly, you dislike their _____. (using *ness,* give the noun form of *ugly*)

- the act of saying
  dict: say
  ion: act of

Still another common noun suffix is *ion*. Someone warns you to watch your *diction* because you are on television. The root is *dict* (say) and the suffix is *ion*. If *ion* means "act of," then *diction* is literally "_____." (Note: Word meanings do change. This literal meaning is a bridge to the current dictionary definition—"the process of choosing words, especially the correct or acceptable words.")

---

*Often as words are formed, letters are dropped or changed, as the e is dropped here. We will focus on the meaning of the new words rather than the spelling.

• **saying ahead of time**	To *predict* something that is going to happen is literally to "say ahead of time." If *ion* is added to this form of the word, you change it to *prediction*, with the meaning "act of _____."
• **rejected**	Sometimes a root itself indicates the part of speech. For example, we need no suffix to tell us that *true* is an adjective. Similarly, *predict* does not contain a suffix, yet it is used as a verb: I *predict* rain for tomorrow. The suffix *ed* is added to form the past tense: I *predicted* rain yesterday. Change the verb *reject* from the present tense to the past tense. _____
• **to think**	A common verb suffix is *ate*, as in *dictate*. There is no literal meaning for *ate*; it simply indicates that the meaning of the word should be cast in the form of a verb: *dict* (say) + *ate* = to say. The verb *cogitate* breaks down into the root *cogit* (think) + *ate* and means "_____." Because *dictate* already ends in the letter
• **cogitated**	*e*, only the letter *d* is needed to make the past tense form: *dictate* + *d* = *dictated*. Form the past tense of *cogitate*. _____
• **ize**	The verb *terrorize* means "to cause terror." If the root is *terror*, then the verb suffix is _____.
• **terrorized**	The past tense of *terrorize* is _____.
• **terrorizing**	To indicate that an action continues to occur, the suffix *ing* is added: The weatherman is *predicting* rain for the weekend. Complete the verb form in the following sentence so that it will mean the action has continued to occur: The monster has been _____ the countryside for four weeks. (use the proper form of *terrorize*)
• **workable**	Adjective word forms are generally indicated by suffixes such as *able*, *ful*, and *ous*. A *capable* (cap + able) man is "able to do" things; material that is "able to be used" is *usable*. A plan that is "able to work" is _____.
• **hazardous**	The adjective suffix *ous* means "marked by." A *courageous* (courage + ous) soldier is "marked by courage." An *advantageous* (advantage + ous) remark is "marked by advantage." Form the word that means "marked by hazard" and could be used to describe road conditions after a storm. _____

- spiteful

The adjective suffix *ful* means "full of." *Helpful* (help + ful) means "full of help"; *harmful* means "full of harm." Form the word that means "full of spite." _____

- purposefully

Adverbial word forms are most commonly indicated by the ending *ly* after roots or after adjective suffixes: tame + ly, helpful + ly. What is the adverbial form of *purposeful?* _____

- routinely

The suffix *ly* can mean the manner in which something is done (He spoke *softly*) or it can show degree (She was *extremely* happy). Fill in the adverbial form of *routine* in the following sentence: Jane did the housework _____.

- unusually

In the following sentence fill in the adverbial form of *unusual* that tells to what degree Harry was sad: "Harry blamed himself for the mistake and felt _____ sad."

- throw forward

Now apply what you have learned to a cluster of words derived from the root *ject*, meaning "throw." Consider the word *project*, as in "Henry tried to *project* a feeling of hope to the crowd." If the prefix *pro* means "forward," then the literal meaning of *project* is "to _____."

- act of throwing forward

Consider the word *projection*, as in "His voice projection was not strong enough." If the suffix *ion* means "act of," then the literal meaning of *projection* is "_____."

- projector

If the suffix *or* means "that which," what word stands for a machine used to "throw forward" images onto a screen? _____

- projectionist

If *ist* means "one who," what word is used to name the person who is responsible for the *projection* of images onto a screen? _____

- projectile

If *ile* is a noun suffix meaning "that which," supply the word that fits the following sentence and means "that which is thrown forward": A bullet is one type of _____ manufactured by this company.

- throw out the patron

A bartender tried to *eject* a misbehaving patron. If *e* means "out," what did the bartender try to do? _____

• ejected

Fill in the past tense form of *eject*: Last evening the bartender _____ three rowdy persons. Fill in the form of *eject* that shows action continuing to occur: The bartender has been

• ejecting

_____ me right after my third drink.

• interject

The prefix *inter* means "between." If you throw a witty remark into a conversation (between other people's remarks), you can be said to _____ it.

• interjection

Bart Simpson is fond of saying "Ay caramba!" This expression conveys emotion rather than thought and gives the impression of being thrown between other lines of dialogue. *Inter* means "between." An expression such as "Ay caramba!" would therefore be called a(n)

_____.

• a guess

"What happened to the money is a matter for *conjecture*." In this sentence, *conjecture* means "that which is thrown together." This literal meaning should lead you to a current dictionary definition. Is *conjecture* a "guess" or a "carefully reasoned explanation"?

_____

• adjective

In the sentence "My remarks about the election are only conjectural," the word *conjectural* describes *remarks* (conjectural remarks). The suffix *al* must therefore indicate a(n) _____ word form.

• adverbial

In the sentence "He spoke conjecturally," the suffix *ly* has been added to *conjectural* and tells the manner in which he spoke. The word *conjecturally* must therefore be a(n) _____ word form.

• heat

Two roots are sometimes combined to form a word, as in *thermometer* (thermo, "heat" + meter, "measure"). *Thermoelectricity* (thermo + electricity) is "electricity produced directly by _____."

• telemeter

If *tele* means "far or distant," an instrument that measures great distances (in space) is called a(n) _____.

SELF-TEST

1. Every word in English must contain a(n) _____ or basic meaning.

2. A word part placed in front of a root to change its meaning is called a(n) _____.

3. In the word *preheat,* the prefix is _____ and the root is _____.

4. More than one prefix can be placed in front of a root. True or False? _____

5. How many prefixes are there in *nonrepayable?* _____

6. A word part placed after a root to indicate the part of speech is called a(n) _____.

7. In the word *dictate,* the suffix is _____.

8. In the word *predictable,* the prefix is _____ , the root is _____ , and the suffix is _____.

9. In which word(s) is *pre* used as a prefix? *predetermine, prey, precious* _____

10. More than one suffix can be placed after a root. True or False? _____

11. In the word *helpfully,* the suffixes are _____ and _____.

12. By adding various prefixes and suffixes, many different words with different meanings can be formed from a single root. True or False? _____

13. *Eject* means "throw out"; *interject* means "throw between"; if *pro* means "forward," *project* means "_____."

14. Two roots can be combined to form a word. True or False? _____

15. The word *thermometer* contains how many roots? _____

ANSWERS   1. root 2. prefix 3. pre/heat 4. True 5. two 6. suffix 7. ate 8. pre/dict/able 9. predeter-mine 10. True 11. ful/ly 12. True 13. throw forward 14. True 15. two

2 Greek Roots

Directions

Begin by reading unit 1. Unit 1, like all the other units in Chapters 2 through 6, is divided into three sections: pronunciation, self-teaching section, and a self-test. For each unit, you should:

1. Study the word part given, paying special attention to its English meaning.

2. Pronounce the words derived from the word part. Say them out loud.

3. Cover the answers at the left side of the self-teaching section with a piece of paper or your hand.

4. Read through the self-teaching section and fill in your answer in each blank provided. The lists at the beginning of each unit contain all the information you will need in the self-teaching section.

5. After you complete each question, check the answer given on the same line in the left column. If you made a mistake, correct it and reread the item to find any clue you overlooked.

6. When you have finished the self-teaching section, go on to the brief unit Self-Test that follows it. Fill in the word or meaning from that unit that best fits the sentence context. When you have finished all the items, check the answers that follow. If you made a mistake, correct it and reread the sentence carefully to find the clue you overlooked. Occasionally you may need to look back at the unit to see how the word was originally defined or used.

1   ANTHROP, ANTHROPO: man, mankind

Prefixes	Other Roots	Suffixes
phil: love	*logy:* study of	*ic, ical:* relating to
	mis: hate	*ist:* one who
	phagus: eater	*oid:* like, resembling
		y: act of

Derivatives   anthropocentric (an thruh puh CEN trik)
anthropophagus (an thruh PAHF uh gus)
anthropological (an thruh puh LODGE uh kuhl)
anthropologist (an thruh PAHL uh just)
anthropology (an thruh PAHL uh gee)
anthropoid (AN thruh poid)
misanthrope (MISS un thrope)
philanthropical (fill un THROP uh kuhl)
philanthropist (fuh LAN thruh puhst)
philanthropy (fuh LAN thruh pee)

- **anthropology**
  anthropo: man
  logy: study of

Margaret Mead was always fascinated with mankind's races, customs, and beliefs. In college she majored in _____. (study of mankind)

- **anthropologist**
  anthropo: man
  logy: study of
  ist: one who

Her field research and book called *Coming of Age in Samoa* made her a famous _____. (one who studies mankind)

- **anthropological**

She tended to view current social problems from a(n) _____ viewpoint or perspective. (related to anthropology)

- **They resemble man; they are man-like.**
  anthrop: man
  oid: resembling

Chimpanzees and gorillas are classified as *anthropoid* apes. What does the word tell you about them? _____.

- **loves**
  phil: love

A *philanthropist* is "one who _____ mankind."

- **philanthropy**

He usually shows this feeling by some form of practical help, such as service to others or a gift of money. The act of showing love in this manner is called _____ .

- **philanthropical**

Charitable enterprises such as soup kitchens and battered women's shelters are called _____ endeavors. (related to philanthropy)

- **he hates mankind**
  mis: hate
  anthrop: man

Scrooge in Dickens's *A Christmas Carol* is a *misanthrope*. How does Scrooge feel toward his fellow man? _____

- **anthropophagus**

A cannibal eats human flesh. So does a man-eater. What is a more academic term? _____.

- **anthropocentric**

What adjective would you use to describe the outlook of a person who considers man to be the most significant thing in the universe—that is, to be the center of it? a(n) _____ outlook.

SELF-TEST

1. His huge donations to worthy causes quickly earned him a reputation as a *philanthropist.* These gifts showed what kind of feeling toward people? _____

2. The TV special featured a young woman who had actually lived for a year among anthropoid apes. *Anthropoid* means _____.

3. Many real estate developers and corporate planners are indifferent about preserving the environment. They concentrate on man and his immediate needs. Their viewpoint is entirely _____. (man-centered)

4. At the moment I am so low on funds that giving you five dollars would have to be considered an act of _____. (act of showing love for mankind)

5. The academic term for "man-eater" is _____.

6. What is a *misanthrope?* A person who _____.

7. *Anthropology* is the _____.

8. Because she traveled with her father when he made his famous studies of North American Indian tribes, Miss Van Pelt considers herself a(n) _____. (one who studies mankind)

9. After a lifetime of stinginess, Mr. Peabody's creation of housing for the poor showed a(n) _____ side. (related to acts of showing love for mankind)

ANSWERS

1. love 2. resembling man (man-like) 3. anthropocentric 4. philanthropy 5. anthropophagus 6. hates people (mankind) 7. study of mankind 8. anthropologist 9. philanthropical

2 ARCH: first, ancient, chief or ruler of government

Prefixes	Other Roots	Suffixes
mon: one	*logy:* study of	*ic:* related to
	olig: few	*ist:* one who
	tect: builder	*y:* state of

Derivatives   archaic (ar KAY ik)
archangel (ARK ain juhl)
archbishop (ARCH BISH up)
archeologist (ar kee AHL uh just)
archeology (ar kee AHL uh gee)
archetype (ARK uh type)
archfiend (ARCH FEEND)
architect (ARK uh tekt)
monarchy (MON ar kee)
oligarchy (AHL uh gar kee)

- **archfiend**

  To rally the country to war, the president portrayed the enemy leader as a(n) _____. (chief fiend)

- **archangel**

  In the Old Testament, Gabriel is a chief angel or _____.

- **ancient; old-fashioned**

  According to some feminists, male courtesies such as opening doors for women are archaic. In this context *archaic* means _____.

- **architect**

  The chief builder in the construction of a building is the _____. (he is also the first builder)

- **a chief one (king or ruler)**

  A *monarchy* is a government controlled by _____.

- **archeology**
  arch: ancient
  logy: study of

  The study of ancient civilizations, carried on particularly by excavating and describing ruins, is called _____.

- **archeologist**

  A person trained to excavate ruins and reconstruct the life of ancient civilizations is called a(n) _____.

- **a chief few; a small group of powerful people**

The economy of the little tropical country was controlled by an oligarchy of plantation owners, military officers, and their friends in the civil service even after the government was overthrown. Who exercises control in an oligarchy? _____

- **the original pattern from which copies were made**

An industrial historian called the Model T Ford the *archetype* of the mass-produced car in America. In this context, which of the following is a better definition? Underline your choice: a very important type/the original pattern from which copies were made.

- **archbishop**

A chief bishop is a(n) _____.

SELF-TEST

1. Because designing a building is the first step in its construction, the person who does it is known as the _____. (chief builder)

2. The builders discovered a slave cemetery while excavating and stopped work while a team of _____ examined it. (those who study ancient civilizations)

3. Recent behavior by Britain's royal family has focused public attention on the _____. (government by one ruler)

4. Doubts about the prince's character have convinced many that this is an _____ (old-fashioned, ancient) institution.

5. The twelve men seized control of the government, and it remained an oligarchy for 21 years. What does *oligarchy* mean? _____

6. As a no-nonsense, straight-shooting, independent-minded movie hero, Clint Eastwood has probably achieved the status of a(n) _____. (chief type)

7. Before the rebellion against heaven, Satan was the most important of the archangels. What does *archangel* mean? _____

8. What is *archeology*? _____

ANSWERS

1. architect 2. archeologists 3. monarchy/archaic 4. rule by a chief few 5. archetype 6. a chief, or top-ranking, angel 7. the study of ancient civilizations 8. one-person rule; government headed by a king or queen

3 CHRON: time

Prefixes	**Other Roots**	**Suffixes**
ana: against	*logy:* study of	*(e)r:* one who
syn: together	*meter:* that which measures	*ic, ical:* relating to
		ism: that which
		ize: verb ending (do what the root says)
		ly: manner of

Derivatives: anachronism (uh NAK run izm)
anachronistic (uh nak run IST ik)
chronic (KRON ik)
chronicle (KRON uh kuhl)
chronicler (KRON uh kler)
chronological (kron uh LODGE uh kuhl)
chronologically (kron uh LODGE uh klee)
chronology (kron AHL uh gee)
chronometer (kruh NOM uh ter)
synchronize (SIN kruh nize)

- **chronic**
  chron: time
  ic: relating to

An illness that lasts over a long period of time is a(n) _____ illness. (relating to time)

- **chronometer**
  chron: time
  meter: that which measures

An extremely accurate clock used in scientific research is called a(n) _____. (that which measures time)

- **together in time**
  syn: together
  chron: time

If two dancers *synchronize* their movements, how do they move? _____

- **anachronism**

After living in the city for so long, I was shocked to see houses in Vermont where doors were left unlocked and windows had no bars on them. Sadly, freedom from fear of crime is a(n) _____.
(that which is against the time sequence; a throwback in time)

- **a throwback in time; against the normal time sequence**

The restaurant celebrated its fiftieth anniversary by serving its original menu at the original prices. People flocked to this *anachronistic* bargain. What does *anachronistic* mean? _____

- **not in the right time order**

A critic reads a biography and claims that the author's *chronology* of data is inaccurate. What does the critic claim about the data? That the data about someone's life is _____.

- **chronological**

In writing a biography you would discuss events in the order in which they occurred; that is, you would discuss them in _____ order. (relating to something based on a time sequence)

- **in a time sequence; in the order they occurred**

The events leading up to the bank robbery were listed *chronologically*. In what manner were the events listed? _____

- **time order; order of occurrence**

A *chronicler* would be a person who records events in what order? _____

- **chronicle**

A historical account that records events in their order of occurrence, usually without interpreting them, is called a(n) _____. (that which is based on time)

SELF-TEST

1. Two packs of cigarettes a day gave him a chronic cough. What does *chronic* mean here? _____

2. It was a(n) _____ to be drinking a can of beer as we stared up at the pyramids. (that which is against the time sequence)

3. The details of Roger's adventure were set forth in _____ order. (relating to time sequence)

4. It would be anachronistic to look out the window and see herds of buffalo grazing on the front lawn! *Anachronistic* means _____.

5. Before hitting the beach, the sergeant told the men to *synchronize* their watches with his. What did he tell them to do? _____

6. The application asked us to list our former jobs *chronologically*. Our formers jobs should be listed in what manner? _____

7. Professor Durio's chief scholarly contribution was to have worked out a reasonably accurate _____ of the known facts about Shakespeare. (discussion based on time sequence)

8. Sir Rounfall's account of the War of the Roses is full of opinion and personal judgment, as he knew; he never claimed to be merely a chronicler. What is a *chronicler*? _____

ANSWERS 1. lasting over a long period of time 2. anachronism 3. chronological 4. relating to a throwback in time 5. set their watches to the same time 6. in the order the jobs were held 7. chronology 8. a person who records events in the order in which they occurred without interpreting them

4 DEM, DEMO: people

Prefixes	Other Roots	Suffixes
en: within	*crac:* rule	*(e)ry:* act of
epi: above, upon, over	*gogue:* leader	*ic:* relating to, being
pan: all	*graph:* record	*y:* act of

Derivatives demagogue (DEM uh gog)
demagoguery (DEM uh gog ree)
democracy (duh MOK ruh see)
demographer (duh MOG ruh fer)
demography (duh MOG ruh fee)
endemic (en DEM ik)
epidemic (ep uh DEM ik)
pandemic (pan DEM ik)

- **people**
demo: people
crac: rule
y: act of

Democracy means rule by the _____.

- **people**
epi: upon
dem: people
ic: relating to

Even though the word *epidemic* means "upon the _____," it is used to describe an outbreak of disease that affects slightly less than ten percent of the population.

- **all**
pan: all
dem: people

- **pandemic**
- **epidemic**

Even though *pandemic* means "_____ the people," it is used to describe an outbreak of disease that affects slightly more than ten percent of the population. Thus, a(n) _____ disease is more widespread than a(n) _____ disease.

- **regularly occurring in a particular people or locality**

You come across a newspaper article that says "the common cold is *endemic* in America." You know that it means "being within a people." Keeping the context and the literal meaning in mind, underline the current meaning you think most likely grew out of it: regularly occurring in a particular people or locality/causing illness to a portion of the people only.

- **endemic**

Character traits may seem to be inborn. Some talk-show hosts believe that incompetence is _____ in government. (being within a people)

- **people leader (leader of people)**

Demagogue means "_____." The word originated at a time when the people were considered to be an ignorant, undiscerning, easily led mob. A demagogue leads people by appealing to their hatreds and prejudices rather than to their idealism and reason. He stirs up people to gain his own ends. If you accused a political candidate or office-holder of demagoguery, would he be insulted or flattered? _____

- **very insulted!**

- **demography**
  demo: people
  graph: record

The "science of recording people" is known as _____.

- **those who collect and study vital statistics . . .**

The U.S. government employs a great many *demographers* who conduct a census of the population every ten years. Given this context and also the literal meaning "those who record people," which do you think is the current meaning of *demographer?* Underline your choice: those who write official letters for people unable to do so for themselves/those who collect and study vital statistics about a people.

SELF-TEST

1. According to the popular notion, thriftiness and frugality are supposed to be endemic to the Scottish. Endemic means _____.

2. A counselor suggested that Mickey might be happy majoring in demography, which is the science of _____.

3. Her talk of a cultural war in America was so full of hate and prejudice and so lacking in logic that she was called a demagogue. A demagogue is _____.

4. Today many advertisers rely heavily on the findings of _____. (those who collect and evaluate statistical data about people)

5. When slightly less than ten percent of the population is suffering from a disease, the public health authorities say it is _____. (upon the people)

6. The senator refused to resort to negative campaigning, rejecting it as _____. (act of leading the people by the wrong methods and principles)

7. In some parts of the country teenage violence has become so wide-spread that it is no longer just epidemic, but instead _____. (being in "all" the people)

8. A one-party system hardly seems suitable if a country really wishes to call itself a(n) _____. (rule by the people)

ANSWERS

1. being within the people; inborn 2. collecting and evaluating data about populations 3. a politician who leads people by their prejudices for his or her own ends 4. demographers 5. epidemic 6. demagoguery 7. pandemic 8. democracy

5   DOX: belief, teaching, opinion

Prefixes	Other Roots	Suffixes
hetero: different	*logy:* words of	*ical:* characterized by
ortho: correct		*ly:* manner of
para: alongside		*y:* state of

Derivatives
doxology (dox AHL uh gee)
heterodox (HET er uh dox)
orthodox (ORTH uh dox)
orthodoxy (ORTH uh dox ee)
paradox (PEAR uh dox)
paradoxical (pear uh DOX uh kuhl)
paradoxically (pear uh DOX ik lee)

• **words of belief**
dox: belief
logy: words of

What is the literal meaning of *doxology?* _____

• **doxology**

A regular feature of some religious services is to sing or recite the _____. (words of belief)

• **the correct belief**
ortho: correct
dox: belief

What is the literal meaning of *orthodox?* _____

• **orthodox**

If your views are within the mainstream, radicals would consider you _____.

• **orthodoxy**

The Surgeon General was asked to resign because her opinions strayed from the social _____. (condition of following correct beliefs)

- **different belief**
  hetero: different
  dox: belief

- **heterodox**

- **paradox**
  para: alongside
  dox: belief

- **paradoxical**

- **paradoxically**

The literal meaning of *heterodox* is being of a(n) _____.

When your opinions differ markedly from the conventional ones, they are labeled _____. (of a different belief)

Suppose there are two equally supportable but contradictory theories to explain what light is. This situation constitutes a(n) _____ (beliefs alongside each other)

The Senator came from one of America's richest families, yet he was a champion of the poor. Columnists of both left and right often call attention to this _____ fact. (relating to beliefs that exist alongside each other)

To phrase it differently, the Senator would have been expected to represent the interests of the wealthy; but _____ he did not. (manner of two beliefs existing alongside each other and contradicting each other)

SELF-TEST

1. The school superintendent believed in the educational basics in an orthodox fashion. That is, she ran her school in what way? _____

2. Elizabeth slipped into a back pew just as the congregation rose to its feet to sing the doxology. Doxology means _____.

3. The American people appear to have _____ natures; one part wants to belong to a group, while another part strongly identifies with the myth of the rugged individualist. (characterized by conflicting beliefs)

4. China is reforming its economy _____. It wants to share in the benefits of international free trade, yet it doesn't want to observe the international copyright laws. (manner of behaving as though one held opposing beliefs)

5. The American Bar Association did not receive Dr. Kramer well because of his heterodox ideas about malpractice insurance. Heterodox means his ideas were _____.

6. In his writing Hawthorne was continually probing the moral paradox that good comes out of evil and evil comes out of good. A paradox is _____.

7. At 18 he was drawn to revolution; at 25 he admitted to some radicalism; at 30 he had completely slipped back into the comfortable lap of political _____. (correct beliefs)

ANSWERS   1. conventionally; based on "correct belief" 2. words of belief 3. paradoxical 4. paradoxically 5. characterized by different beliefs; unconventional 6. an apparent contradiction of beliefs 7. orthodoxy

6   DYNA: power

Other Roots   **Suffixes**
thermo: heat   *ic:* being, relating to
                          ics: operation of

Derivatives   dynamic (deye NAM ik)
                   dynamics (deye NAM iks)
                   dynamite (DEYE nuh mite)
                   dynamo (DEYE nuh mo)
                   dynasty (DEYE nuss tee)
                   thermodynamics (THUR mo deye NAM iks)

• **being powerful or effective**

The coach was so *dynamic* when addressing an audience that he made a lot of money in the off season as a motivational speaker. What does *dynamic* mean here? _____

• **power**

The school psychologist wrote her thesis on the dynamics of interpersonal relationships. Literally, *dynamics* would be "the operation of _____." This literal meaning leads to the current definition: "the physical or moral forces at work in any field."

• **dyna**

The bridge was blown up with dynamite. What part of the word *dynamite* tells you that it is an explosive of great power for force?

_____

• **power (energy)**

At Hoover Dam each dynamo generates an incredible amount of electrical energy each day. If *dyna* can also mean "energy," then a *dynamo* is "that which generates _____." A fuller definition is "a machine that generates electricity by changing mechanical energy into electrical energy." A person who is extremely energetic ("a real live wire") can also be called a(n) _____.

• **dynamo**

• **heat and power (electrical energy)**

In a branch of physics called *thermodynamics,* you study the relation between what forces? _____

SELF-TEST

1. After overcoming her early shyness, Thelma later became a famous and dynamic actress. Dynamic here means _____.

2. The Yankees won so many championships over so many years that the team was known as the Yankee _____.

3. Martha Stewart has mastered so many domestic arts, such as cooking, gardening, and shopping, and she has so many publishing and other media ventures, that people wonder where she gets the energy to do it all. She is a human _____. (that which generates power)

4. Roger said he had seen at first hand the _____ at work in the selection of a presidential candidate. (physical or moral forces at work in a field)

5. An old building of that type would have to be destroyed with _____. (explosive of great power or force)

6. Her brother, whose interests lay in physics, specialized in thermo-dynamics. What is thermodynamics? _____

ANSWERS

1. powerful or effective 2. dynasty 3. dynamo 4. dynamics 5. dynamite 6. a branch of physics dealing with the relation between heat and electrical energy (power)

7 GAM: marriage

Prefixes	Other Roots	Suffixes
bi: two	*miso:* hate	*ist:* one who
en: within		*ous:* based on
exo: outside		*y:* act
mono: one		
poly: many		

Derivatives
bigamist (BIG uh mist)
bigamy (BIG uh mee)
endogamy (en DOG uh mee)
exogamy (egg ZOG uh mee)
misogamist (mih SOG uh mist)
monogamist (muh NOG uh mist)
monogamous (muh NOG uh muss)
monogamy (muh NOG uh mee)
polygamy (puh LIG uh mee)

- **only one**
  mono: one
  gam: marriage
  ist: one who

A *monogamist* enters into how many marriages at the same time? _____

- **monogamous**

A reasonably conventional person will seek to establish a(n) _____ relationship with a mate. (based on one marriage at a time)

- **monogamy**

A monogamist believes in or practices _____. (act of having one marriage)

- **bigamy**
  bi: two
  gam: marriage
  y: act

In our culture a person caught being married to two or more people at the same time is guilty of _____. (act of having two marriages)

- **bigamist**

In fact, newspaper reporters will label such a person a(n) _____. (one who has two or more marriages at the same time)

- **polygamy**

Some cultures allow a person to have more than one marriage at a time. When legal, such a practice is called _____. (act of many marriages)

- **endogamy**

Too many marriages within the same group can lead to physical defects. If *endo* means "within," another name for inbreeding is _____.

- **exogamy**

To maintain the vigor of the race, some groups require that young men take brides outside their own group, a practice called _____.

- **a person who hates marriage**

What is a misogamist? _____

SELF-TEST

1. The marriage code of the Western nations is based on monogamy. That is, the code is based on _____.

2. In some parts of Africa wealthy men are not only allowed, but also are encouraged to practice polygamy. Polygamy is _____.

3. Thinking to discourage her pursuit of him, Mr. Jones said, "Please, Miss Tuttle! I am a(n) _____!" (one who practices one marriage at a time)

4. The old bachelor readily admitted that he was a misogamist. What did he admit to? _____

5. His Mexican divorce was ruled invalid, and the court held that he was technically guilty of bigamy when he married his second wife, Susan. That is, he was guilty of _____.

6. Marriage inside one's own family or group is called

_____.

1. having only one marriage at a time 2. act of having many marriages at the same time 3. monogamist 4. hating marriage 5. having two wives at the same time 6. endogamy

8 GEN: birth, race, kind

Prefixes
con: with
de: reverse of
pro: forward

Other Roots
cide: kill
logy: study of
photo: light
psych: mind

Suffixes
al: that which
al: being
ate: verb ending
ist: one who
or: one who
us: that which
y: result of

Derivatives
congenital (kuhn JEN ih tuhl)
degenerate (dee JEN er ate)
gene (JEEN)
genealogist (jeen ee AHL uh just)
genealogy (jeen ee AHL uh gee)
generate (JEN er ate)
genitals (JEN uh tulls)
genocide (JEN uh side)
genus (GEE nuss)
photogenic (fote uh JEN ik)
progenitor (pro JEN uh ter)
progeny (PRAH jen ee)
psychogenic (seye ko JEN ik)

• birth, race, or kind

The chemical units that carry hereditary characteristics from parents to offspring are called genes. *Genes,* then, determine the characteristics of _____.

• congenital
  con: with
  gen: birth
  al: being

A defect that is present "with birth" is said to be _____.

• they gave you birth, sent you forward into the world or future

What do you think it means to say that your parents, grandparents, and great-grandparents are your *progenitors?* _____

• it gives birth to excitement

If a new piece of music *generates* excitement, what does it do? _____

• worse

If a plant or animal strain *degenerates,* does it become better or worse? _____

• photogenic

Which of the derivatives might describe a person who looks good in photographs? _____

• race or kind

The *genitals* are the sexual organs that reproduce the _____.

• race
  gen: race
  cide: kill

Genocide is the intentional destruction of a(n) _____, but it can be extended to include social or political groups.

• genus

Botanists not only describe each plant as being a particular species but also classify it as a member of a larger family (kind) of plants known as a genus. For example, the Easter lily is known botanically as *lilium longiflorum,* and it belongs to the _____ *liliaceae.* (family of plants)

• a person who traces family origins

The television movie "Roots" inspired many people to consult genealogists to work out their family trees. What is a genealogist? _____

• **genealogy**   What is the study of family pedigrees called? _____

• **birth**   Literally, *progeny* means something like "that which has been given
_____." More simply, progeny are the offspring of
plants or animals.

• **psychogenic**   All illness that appears to have been produced or created by a mental
condition is said to be _____. (having its origin in the
mind)

SELF-TEST

1. My cousin, an amateur genealogist, traced our family to a village in
   Russia. What does a genealogist do? _____

2. The so-called meadow cowslip is primula vulgaris, which belongs to
   the _____ primulaceae. (family or kind)

3. Because they killed everyone in the town of Lidice, the Nazis were
   accused of genocide. Genocide means _____.

4. The Smiths' oldest son is afflicted with a(n) _____
   speech defect. (present at birth)

5. Your parents and grandparents are your _____.
   (those who gave you birth, sent you forth)

6. Some kinds of migraine headache are thought to be psychogenic in
   nature. Psychogenic means _____.

7. Lawrence was so tired he said he must have _____
   for laziness. (chemical units that carry hereditary characteristics)

8. Aunt Matilda always hides when it comes time for picture-taking. She
   says she is not photogenic. Photogenic means _____.

9. The TV show "LA Law" generated new interest among students in
   going to law school. This means that interest in law: increased/
   decreased/remained the same.

10. Because she had been adopted, Mary could not trace her
    _____. (family origins)

ANSWERS   1. traces family origins 2. genus 3. murder of a race or group 4. congenital 5. progenitors
6. originating in the mind 7. genes 8. looks good in photographs 9. increased 10. genealogy

9   HYDR: water

Other Roots
phobia: fear
phyte: plant
ponics: labor
therapy: cure, treatment

Suffixes
ant: that which
ic: relating to
ly: manner of

Derivatives
hydrant (HEYE drunt)
hydraulic (heye DRAW lik)
hydrophobia (heye dro FOE bee uh)
hydrophyte (HEYE dro fite)
hydroplane (HEYE dro plane)
hydroponically (heye dro PON ik lee)
hydroponics (heye dro PON iks)
hydrotherapy (heye dro THER uh pee)

- **water**

A fire *hydrant* is a large outlet for _____.

- **hydroplane**

A plane that can land or take off on water is a(n) _____.

- **water**

A *hydraulic* press is operated by _____ pressure.

- **a water plant**
  hydr: water
  phyte: plant

What is a *hydrophyte?* _____

- **the use of water as a treatment**

What is *hydrotherapy?* _____

- **water fear**
  hydr: water
  phobia: fear

The technical term for rabies is *hydrophobia.* The literal meaning of *hydrophobia* is "_____." A victim of this disease exhibits a morbid fear of water because of the inability to swallow water or liquids.

- **hydroponics**

The science of growing plants in water instead of soil is called _____. (water labor)

- **hydroponically**

Many vegetables and flowers are now being produced _____. (in a manner based on water labor)

SELF-TEST

1. Most American cars now employ hydraulic rather than mechanical brakes. Hydraulic brakes use what kind of pressure?
   _____

2. The hyacinths that choke irrigation ditches and rice paddies are examples of undesirable hydrophytes. What is a hydrophyte?
   _____

3. The doctor prescribed _____ for baseball pitchers after the game, so they always soaked their arms in the whirlpool bath. (use of water as a cure or treatment)

4. In Scandinavia, hydroponics have provided a steady supply of fresh vegetables during the long, dark winters. Plants grown hydroponically are grown in _____.

5. Small _____ bring mail, food, and supplies to these lonely Alaskan settlements. ("water planes")

6. The traffic ticket irritated her because she thought she had parked far enough away from the fire _____. (large water outlet)

ANSWERS   1. water pressure 2. water plant 3. hydrotherapy 4. water 5. hydroplanes 6. hydrant

10   LOG, LOGY: speech, study of, collection of

Prefixes	Other Roots	Suffixes
dia: across	*astro:* star	*ic:* science of
mono: one	*crypt:* secret	*ical:* relating to
	ichthy: fish	
	ideo: idea	
	mania: madness	
	orn: bird	
	tech: trade, skill	
	zoo: animal	

Derivatives   astrology (ass TRAHL uh gee)
cryptology (krip TAHL uh gee)
ichthyology (ik thee AHL uh gee)
ideological (id ee uh LODGE uh kuhl)
ideology (id ee AHL uh gee)
logic (LODGE ik)

logomania (log oh MAIN ee uh)
monologue (MON uh log)
ornithology (orn uh THAHL uh gee)
technology (tek NAHL uh gee)
travelogue (TRAV uh log)
zoology (zoe AHL uh gee)

- **monologue**
  mono: one
  log: speech

  When two actors speak to each other across a stage, we say they are carrying on a dialogue. When one actor speaks alone on the stage, we call it a(n) _____. ("speech across")

- **travelogue**

  Which derivative means a lecture, often with illustrations, about visiting part of the world? _____

  Sherlock Holmes used *logic* to solve crimes. The literal meaning of *logic*—the science of words—provides little help unless you realize that words are used in reasoning.

- **reasoning**

  In an effort to prove something by *logic,* you would use _____.

- **logomania**
  log: speech
  mania: madness

  Which derivative would mean abnormal talkativeness? _____ (a madness for speech)

  Logy also means "study of." For example, *biology* is the "study of life" and *psychology* is the "study of the mind." What is the meaning of the derivatives below?

- **study of animals**

  zoology _____

- **study of birds**

  ornithology _____

- **study of fishes**

  ichthyology _____ (both ornithology and ichthyology are branches of zoology)

- **study of stars**

  astrology _____

  Astrology should be distinguished from *astronomy. Astrology* remains a study of stars to read character and forecast events. This is considered by most scientists to be a pseudo-science, which means "false science." *Astronomy,* which means "systematized knowledge of the stars," is a true science.

- **astrology**

  An *astrologer* would give you a *horoscope*, or prediction about your future, based on: *astrology/astronomy*.

- **astronomer**

  Who would tell you when a comet was likely to collide with the earth? _____

- **cryptology**

  What derivative means "the study of secret messages"? _____

- **collection of ideas that constitute a person's point of view**

  Logy can also mean "collection of." What do we mean when we talk of a person's ideology? _____

- **ideological**

  If two people have quite different points of view, we say they have _____ differences. (relating to a collection of ideas)

- **technology**

  Which derivative means a collection of skills required to carry on industry? _____

SELF-TEST

1. Much of the credit for the Allied victory in World War II belonged not to soldiers, but to the Allied _____ experts who broke the German codes. (the study of hidden messages)

2. During the Cold War, the world was divided politically along _____ lines, between Communist and non-Communist countries.

3. Before her guests appeared, the talk-show host began every show with a(n) _____.

4. His gift for sketching and his hobby of bird-watching naturally led him into the field of _____. (study of birds)

5. The ex-president's wife used astrology to help plan her husband's travel schedule. What is astrology? _____

6. Many screenwriters and directors were blacklisted by the movie industry because they were suspected of being left-wingers who included _____ messages in their work. (relating to a collection of ideas)

7. Perry Mason is noted for the kind of _____ he used in proving the innocence of his clients. (reasoning with words)

8. A person who has logomania is _____.

9. One reason for the rising cost of health care is expensive investment in new medical _____. (collection of skills needed in industry)

10. Nevin had studied enough _____ to be able to classify most of the creatures living in or near the pond. (study of animals)

1. cryptology 2. ideological 3. monologue 4. ornithology 5. study of the stars for prediction and character reading 6. ideological 7. logic 8. abnormally talkative 9. technology 10. zoology

11 MEGA, MEGALO: great
MICRO: small

Other Roots	Suffixes
be: life	*iac:* one who
cosm: universe	
mania: madness	
meter: measure	
phone: sound	
polis: city	

Derivatives

megabyte (MEG uh bite)
megaphone (MEG uh phone)
megalomania (meg uh lo MAIN ee uh)
megalomaniac (meg uh lo MAIN ee ak)
megalopolis (meg uh LOP uh liss)
megaton (MEG uh tuhn)
megavitamin (MEG uh VITE uh muhn)
microbe (MY krobe)
microchip (MY kro chip)
microcosm (MY kro kozm)
microfilm (MY kro film)
micrometer (my KROM uh ter)
microorganism (my kro OR guh nizm)

• **increase the loudness of the voice**

To help their voices carry farther, cheerleaders sometimes use *megaphones*. What do you think these instruments do? _____

• megalomania	To have an abnormal desire to do great things is to suffer from _____. (madness about doing great things)
• megalomaniac	A person who suffers such an abnormality is a(n) _____.
• megaton	An atomic bomb with an explosive force equal to one million tons of dynamite would have a value of one _____. ("great ton")
• megalopolis	A great concentration of population, usually identified by its largest city, is called a(n) _____.
• microchips and microprocessors	The invention of _____ and _____ allowed engineers to greatly reduce the size of computers.
• microwave	The _____ oven has made food preparation much more convenient.
• microorganisms	Tiny germs or bacteria that cannot be seen except through a microscope are called _____.
• microbes	They can also be called _____. (small life)
• measures very small things	A micrometer is an instrument that is often used with a microscope. What do you think a scientist does with a *micrometer*? _____
• megavitamin	A great dose of vitamins—one many times the minimum daily requirement—is called a(n) _____.
• "small universe"	*Microcosm* means "_____."
• a representation in miniature	Our troubled school is a microcosm of the larger society. What is a microcosm?_____

SELF-TEST

1. Many people who have studied him believe that General MacArthur was a(n) _____. (one with an abnormal desire to do great things)

2. The terrorists developed a one-_____ bomb and were caught smuggling it to the United States.

3. A virus is a disease-producing agent smaller than any known _____. (either of two words fits here)

4. Most visitors think of the Greater Los Angeles Area as being a megalopolis. A megalopolis is _____.

5. Rudy Vallee, a popular singer during the twenties, sang through a megaphone, which is a(n) _____.

6. A single drop of water from a pond, examined under the microscope, appears to be a microcosm of the biological laws affecting all life. What is a microcosm? _____

7. Some people think that megavitamin doses can prevent or cure cancer. Megavitamins refers to _____.

8. Today's video games are more powerful than yesterday's supercomputers because of the use of _____. (tiny chips or processors)

ANSWERS   1. megalomaniac 2. megaton 3. microorganisms or microbes 4. a large concentration of population 5. a hornlike instrument for increasing sound 6. a small universe; a representation in miniature 7. large doses of vitamins, beyond the daily requirement 8. microchips or microprocessors

12 MORPH: form

Prefixes	Other Roots	Suffixes
a: without	*anthropo:* man	*ic:* relating to
meta: change	*poly:* many	*ism:* act of
	logy: study of	*osis:* process
		ous: relating to, being

Derivatives amorphous (uh MOR fuss)
anthropomorphic (an thruh puh MOR fik)
anthropomorphism (an thruh puh MORF izm)
metamorphosis (met uh MORF uh sis)
morphology (mor FAHL uh gee)
polymorphic (pahl uh MOR fik)
polymorphous (pahl uh MOR fuss)

• **process of change in form**
meta: change
morph: form
osis: process

Caterpillars undergo a metamorphosis to become butterflies. The word parts tell us that *metamorphosis* means _____.

- **without form**
  a: without
  morph: form
  ous: being

If your plans or ideas about something are *amorphous*, that means they are _____.

- **form**

Some people worship *anthropomorphic* deities. These are gods conceived in the _____ of man.

- **anthropomorphism**

People who treat their pets like people are also said to be practicing _____. (act of turning things into the form of man)

- **the form and structure**

If a geologist, a linguist, or a biologist is studying *morphology*, each is studying what part of his subject? _____.

- **different forms**

If an organism or a substance is *polymorphic* or *polymorphous*, that means it has, occurs in, or assumes _____.

SELF-TEST

1. John's vacation plans are amorphous. What does that tell us about John's vacation plans? _____

2. Weightlifting and steroids brought about his _____ from a shy, skinny boy into an aggressive, muscular brute. (process of changing form)

3. An organism that occurs in or assumes many forms can be described with two adjectives: _____ or _____.

4. When the actress started instructing visitors to bring her miniature poodle gifts and shake hands with it, her friends decided her anthropomorphic behavior had gone too far and that she was having a nervous breakdown. Anthropomorphic means _____.

5. The crude carvings of man-like dogs and cats were evidence of _____. (noun form of *anthropomorphic*)

6. A branch of biology called morphology deals with the _____ of plants and animals.

ANSWERS   1. they are unformed or vague 2. metamorphosis 3. polymorphic or polymorphous 4. in the form of man 5. anthropomorphism 6. form and structure

13   NEO: new

Other Roots	Suffixes
lith: stone	*ic, ical:* relating to
logism: word	
phyte: plant	

Derivatives

neoclassical (knee uh KLASS uh kuhl)
neocolonialism (knee uh kuh LONE ee uhl izm)
neolithic (knee uh LITH ik)
neologism (knee OL uh jiz um)
neonatal (KNEE oh NA tuhl)
neophyte (KNEE uh fite)

- **new plant**
  neo: new
  phyte: plant

A *neophyte* is a(n) "_____," but the word is used to identify a person newly initiated into something.

- **new stone**
  new: new
  lith: stone

The *neolithic* period, a time when primitive man advanced to using polished stone tools, literally means the _____ age.

- **new word**
  neo: new
  logism: word

Ten years ago, *yuppie* was a *neologism.* What does *neologism* mean? _____

- **neoclassical**

During the late seventeenth and early eighteenth centuries, many English artists and authors turned to the classical works of ancient Greece and Rome for their inspiration. This period is known as the _____ age. (new classical)

- **neocolonialism**

If a large nation follows a policy of trying to dominate former colonies politically or economically, this practice is called _____. (new colonialism)

SELF-TEST

1. The stone knife dated back to the neolithic period. Neolithic means _____.

2. Maria eventually became a fine seamstress and an efficient housekeeper, but she cooked like a(n) _____. ("new plant")

3. "Uptight" and similar neologisms usually have a life span of about 20 years. What is a neologism? _____

4. Mexican politicians restricted United States investment because they feared economic _____.

5. Almost every American town has its _____ architecture, usually a bank with marble columns right in the middle of Main Street.

ANSWERS   1. new stone 2. neophyte 3. new word 4. neocolonialism 5. neoclassical

14   NOM: rule, law, systematized knowledge

Other Roots	Suffixes
agr: field	*er:* one who
astro: star	*ic:* relating to
auto: self	*ically:* in a manner relating to
metro: measure	*ist:* one who
	ous: being
	y: state of, act of

Derivatives

agronomist (uh GRAHN uh mist)
agronomy (uh GRAHN uh mee)
astronomer (uh STRON uh mer)
astronomic (ass truh NOM ik)
astronomically (ass truh NOM ik lee)
astronomy (uh STRON uh mee)
autonomous (aw TAHN uh muss)
autonomy (aw TAHN uh mee)
metronome (MET ro nome)

• **metronome**

A clocklike device with a pendulum that can be adjusted to tick (keep time) at different speeds is a(n) _____. (that which "rules the measure")

• **self-rule**
auto: self
nom: rule
y: state of

Many countries once dominated by the former Soviet Union have achieved *autonomy*—that is, they have achieved _____.

• **autonomous**

A local school system that wishes to be completely free of interference from county, state, or federal officials wishes to be _____.
(relating to self-rule)

• **agronomy**

The management of crop production is called _____.
("rule of the field")

• **agronomist**

Many farmers who can't get high prices for their usual crops hire an _____ to help them figure out what to grow instead.
(one who manages crop production)

• **astronomy**
  astro: star
  nom: systematized knowledge

What field would you study to gain a systematized knowledge of the stars? _____

• **astronomer**

You may recall from an earlier unit that a scientist who "studies the stars" is a(n) _____.

• **astronomic**

The study of the stars involves fantastically high numbers. In mathematics, we describe high numbers as being _____.
(relating to knowledge of the stars)

• **prices are fantastically high**

If we say that the national debt has risen *astronomically,* what do we mean? _____

SELF-TEST

1. Some nonprofit organizations find that accepting public funds comes with too many strings attached and that they want greater _____ in running their programs than the government allows.

2. Countries that suffer from famine send students to American universities to study agronomy. What will they study? _____

3. The cost of health care rose _____ during the 1980s.
(in a manner involving fantastically high figures)

4. The Hubble telescope is a boon to _____. (those who have systematized knowledge of the stars)

5. Although considered part of the larger educational educational system, each of the four colleges is fully _____. (self-governing)

6. Larry always used a metronome when he practiced the piano. What does the metronome do? _____

7. The soil on our farm was tested by a(n) _____. (one who manages crop production)

8. The study of the stars used to predict human events is called astrology; the scientific study of the stars is called _____.

1. autonomy 2. crop management 3. astronomically 4. astronomers 5. autonomous
6. it keeps time 7. agronomist 8. astronomy

14 ONYM: name

Prefixes
a: without
acro: tip
ant: opposite
hetero: different
homo: same
patr: father
pseudo: false
syn: together

Suffixes
ity: state of
ly: (adverbial ending) manner of

• **false name**
pseudo: false
onym: name

Many authors write under a "pen name" or pseudonym. Pseudonym literally means _____.

• **synonyms**

Calm and *peaceful* mean almost the same thing; they are called _____. ("together words")

• **opposite**
ant: opposite
onym: name

Calm and *troubled* are *antonyms*. That is, their meanings are _____.

• **acronym**

PAC (political action committee) is a word formed from the initials (tips) of other words. Such a word, or the name of an organization like NASA (National Aeronautics and Space Administration), is called a(n) _____.

- **father name**
  patr: father
  onym: name

When a surname like Johnson is derived from the name of the father, it is called a patronym. *Patronym* literally means _____.
(Johnson = the son of John)

- **homonyms**

Sea and *see* are spelled differently and have different meanings, yet they are pronounced the same. This characteristic allows them to be classified as _____. ("same words")

- **different words**

Wind (to twist) and *wind* (air in motion) are spelled the same, but have different meanings. Because they are pronounced differently, they are classified as *heteronyms*, which means _____.

- **without a name**
  a: without
  onym: name

A letter without a name signed to it is an *anonymous* letter. It is literally _____.

- **anonymously**

If you wished to donate to a charity without identifying yourself, you would do so in what manner? _____ (without giving a name)

- **anonymity**

When they travel, some movie stars simply put on dark glasses and hope that people who recognize them will respect their desire for _____. (state of being without a name; being unidentified)

1. Mark Twain was the _____ used by one of America's greatest writers, Samuel Langhorne Clemens. (false name; pen name)

2. If a journalist cites an anonymous source, why will some readers not believe the story?

3. Cite, sight, and site are frequently confused because they are _____. (the same words; words pronounced the same)

4. We ought to call our organization something like Society of Amateur Psychologists so that we could use the _____ SOAP.

5. Bass (a fish) and bass (a male voice) are _____. (different words; words pronounced differently)

6. Mr. Worthington donated large sums of money to the college _____. (in a manner based on not giving his name)

7. Love and hate are _____. (opposite words)

8. Hate and detest are _____. (together words; words with similar meaning)

9. Swenson (the son of Swen) is a(n) _____. (surname based on the father's name)

10. The newspaper protected the _____ of the rape victim. (lack of identification)

ANSWERS

1. pseudonym 2. because unidentified sources can't be questioned about what they say. 3. homonyms 4. acronym 5. heteronyms 6. anonymously 7. antonyms 8. synonyms 9. patronym 10. anonymity

16 PAN: all

Other Roots
cea: cure
chrom: color
demon: devil
orama: view
ply: arms
the: god

Suffixes
atic: marked by
ism: theory, practice; belief

Derivatives
panacea (pan uh SEE uh)
Pan-American
panchromatic (pan kro MAT ik)
pandemonium (pan duh MOAN ee um)
panoply (PAN uh plee)
panorama (pan uh RAM uh)
pantheism (PAN thee izm)
pantheon (PAN thee ahn)

• **all**

The *Pan*-American Highway extends through _____ the countries that border the Pacific Ocean.

• **all colors**
pan: all
chrom: color

Something that is *panchromatic* is sensitive to _____.

- **cure-all**
  pan: all
  cea: cure

- **panaceas**

- **panacea**

Something supposedly able to cure all kinds of medical or political problems is a panacea. *Panacea* means _____.
Patent medicines that promise to cure a wide variety of ailments are _____. A political program that is offered as a cure for all kinds of social and economic problems is also a(n) _____. (They may not cure anything at all; they make you feel good temporarily because they contain so much alcohol!)

- **all the devils**
  pan: all
  demon: devil

Shouting "Fire!" in a crowded theatre can create *pandemonium*. When people panic, they behave as though what had been let loose? _____

- **pantheon**

The Pantheon in Greece was a temple for all the gods. Today we extend the meaning to a building commemorating heroes. For example, the Baseball Hall of Fame is the _____ for baseball players.

- **a complete or unbroken view**

What would someone mean if he said that around the next bend in the road there would be a *panorama* of the city? _____

- **pantheism**

To believe that God is identical with the universe and is all-embracing is to believe in _____. (belief that everything that exists is God)

- **he appears in robes or other special clothing (from early days)**

A knight who arrived on the field of battle in full *panoply* wore a complete suit of armor. Today when a prime minister appears in the full panoply of office, what do you think is meant? _____

SELF-TEST

1. The company's profits soared when it first introduced _____ film for home cameras. (sensitive to all colors)

2. A "return to family values" may be a good thing, but it sounds suspiciously like a panacea for social ills. A panacea is _____.

3. Native American tribes gather there once a year in their full panoply of paint and feathers. Panoply is _____.

4. Their concept of God is confusing to us: to them He is present everywhere, at all times. Their religious belief seems more like what we would call _____. (belief that everything that exists is God)

5. Releasing the mouse on the tea table caused _____ at the Friday Afternoon Bridge Club. ("all the demons"; a wild uproar)

6. The 50-foot-long mural was a panorama of the old days on the Mississippi River. A panorama is _____.

7. The ancient Greek temple built to honor all the gods was called the _____.

8. Games participated in by all the countries of the Americas would be called _____ games. ("all-American")

1. panchromatic 2. a cure-all 3. robes or other special clothing 4. pantheism 5. pandemonium 6. a wide or unbroken view 7. Pantheon 8. Pan-American

17 PATH: feeling, suffering, disease

Prefixes	Other Roots	Suffixes
a: without	*logy:* study of	*ic:* characterized by
anti: against	*osteo:* bones	*ist:* one who
em: inside, within	*psycho:* mind	*y:* act of, quality of, capacity of
sym: with, together		

Derivatives
antipathy (ann TIP uh thee)
apathy (AP uh thee)
empathy (EM puh thee)
osteopath (OSS tee uh path)
pathetic (puh THET ik)
pathologist (puh THAHL uh just)
pathology (puh THAHL uh gee)
pathos (PAY thahss)
psychopath (SEYE koe path)
sympathy (SIM puh thee)

• **act of feeling with**
 sym: with
 path: feeling

• **sympathy**

• **empathy**
 em: inside
 path: feeling

Your ability to be moved by another person's problems is called *sympathy*, which literally means _____. Sympathy is the capacity to share someone else's suffering. You would express _____ to a friend who had lost a loved one.

A more complete identification with another's feelings is called _____. (act of being inside the feeling)

Empathy is imaginative identification with someone else's feelings, ideas, or motives. For example, a baby nursing at its mother's breast may react with a stomach upset if the mother is frightened. Or a spectator might so identify with a boxer that he reacts bodily to blows that hit the boxer.

- **dislike**

Mr. Jones was quickly aware of Joan's *antipathy*. Does Joan like or dislike Mr. Jones? _____ You can prove your answer by knowing that antipathy means literally "a state of _____."

- **feeling against**
  anti: against
  path: feeling

- **unconcerned**

No one could understand John's *apathy* about his family's troubles. Did John appear interested or did he seem unconcerned? _____ You can prove your answer by knowing that *apathy* means literally "a state of being _____."

- **without feeling**
  a: without
  path: feeling

- **suffering**

One of the meanings of *path* is "suffering." A *pathetic*-looking person pears to be _____, and he therefore arouses in us a feeling of pity.

When this feeling of pity is aroused in speech, writing, art, or music, it is given the name *pathos*.

- **pathos**

For example, Shakespeare's serious plays present us with the spectacle of good men suffering and call forth our compassion. They contain the quality of _____.

- **pathology**
  path: disease
  logy: study of

Path also means "disease." The study of unhealthy conditions and processes caused by disease is called _____.

- **pathologist**

Tissue that is suspected of being cancerous should be examined by a(n) _____. (one who studies diseases, especially those leading to death)

- **bones**
  osteo: bones
  path: disease

An *osteopath* treats diseases by manipulating the _____ and muscles.

- **mind**
  psycho: mind
  path: disease

If you say that someone is neurotic, you mean he is too nervous; but if you say that someone is a *psychopath,* you mean he has a disease of the

_____. A *psychopath* has a mental condition bordering on insanity.

SELF-TEST

1. When sympathy turns into the stronger feeling of empathy, a therapist can begin to see the world from the patient's point of view. Empathy means _____.

2. The pattern of stalking the victims and the brutality of the crimes indicates that the killer may be a psychopath. This means that the killer: has a diseased mind/is an adolescent/is very religious.

3. She looked so _____ standing out there in the pouring rain that I asked her to come in and dry herself by the fire. (marked by suffering)

4. The study of abnormalities of the body, particularly those brought on by disease, is called _____. ("study of disease")

5. I am not worth bothering about; save your _____. (act of sharing or "feeling with" someone else's suffering)

6. Prolonged malnutrition had produced in the prisoners a state of apathy, which is a condition of being _____.

7. The hospital pathologist said that he could not determine the precise time of death. A pathologist is _____.

8. The voters seem to have less _____ for the poor than they did 20 years ago. (feeling of pity)

9. It seemed that everything the president did aroused the antipathy of Congress. Antipathy means _____.

ANSWERS

1. being inside the feeling; identifying with someone 2. has a diseased mind 3. pathetic 4. pathology 5. sympathy 6. without feeling 7. one who studies abnormalities brought on by disease 8. sympathy 9. dislike; feeling against

18

PHIL: love

Other Roots	**Suffixes**
adelph: brother	*e:* one who
bibl: book	*er:* one who, that which
harmonia: music	*ic:* marked by
soph: wisdom	*ist:* one who

Derivatives   Anglophile (ANG lo file)
bibliophile (BIB lee uh file)
Francophile (FRANK oh file)
Philadelphia (fill uh DELL fee uh)
philanderer (fuh LAN der er)
philatelist (fuh LAT uh lust)
philharmonic (fill har MON ik)
philosopher (fuh LOSS uh fer)
philter, philtre (FILL ter)

• **philosopher**
   phil: love
   soph: wisdom

If *soph* means "wisdom," one who loves wisdom and searches for it is a(n) _____.

• **love**

A *philharmonic* society is formed by people who _____ music.

• **one who loves
   books**

What is a *bibliophile?* _____

• **a loving man**

A *philanderer* is what kind of man? _____.
The problem is that he makes love to women without having serious intentions.

• **love**

A *philter (philtre)* is a drug or potion used to make a person fall in _____.

• **a person who loves
   all aspects of the
   French culture**

If an *Anglophile* is a person who loves all aspects of the English culture, what is a *Francophile?* _____

• **Philadelphia**

If *adelph* means "brother," what famous American city has a name that means "brotherly love"? _____

• **philatelist**

The root *ately* originally signified a stamp showing that a tax had been paid. Today a person who likes to collect and study stamps is called a(n) _____.

SELF-TEST

1. Calling a man a Don Juan is virtually the same as calling him a philanderer. What is a philanderer? _____

2. Jeff has carefully saved every book he has read since childhood—the mark of a(n) _____. (book lover)

3. The young prince was always reading, questioning his tutors, and embarrassing his father with questions about honor and justice. The old king shook his head sadly and admitted to himself that the next king would no doubt be a philosopher. A philosopher is one who

   _____.

4. Because the community was so far removed from a large urban center, Mr. Bowles suggested that all of us music lovers form our own _____ society. (marked by love of harmony)

5. The old gypsy swore she had a philter that, when added to a man's drink, would cause him to do what? _____

6. My daughter, who encourages me to bring home from the office all the discarded envelopes, is a philatelist. What is a philatelist?

   _____

ANSWERS   1. someone who makes love without serious intentions 2. bibliophile 3. loves wisdom
4. philharmonic 5. fall in love 6. stamp collector

19 POD, PED: foot
PED: child

Prefixes	**Other Roots**	**Suffixes**
bi: two	*agogy:* leading	*cian:* one who
cent: hundred	*phile:* lover	*ist:* one who
mil: thousand		*y:* act of
quadr: four		
tri: three		

Derivatives   biped (BEYE ped)
centipede (SENT uh peed)
millipede (MILL uh peed)
pedagogue (PED uh gog)
pedagogy (PED uh go gee)
pedal (PED uhl)
pedestal (PED us tuhl)
pediatrician (PEED ee uh TRISH un)
pedophile (PEE do file)
podiatrist (poe DEYE uh trist)
quadruped (QUAD rue ped)
tripod (TREYE pod)

• **three**
  tri: three
  pod: foot

A *tripod* is a stand used to hold a camera steady. How many legs does the tripod have? _____

• **biped**

Man walks erect on two feet; he is therefore classified as a(n) _____. The four-legged horse he rides is a(n)

• **quadruped**

_____.

• **100**

A *centipede* is an insect with many pairs of legs. How many legs does it seem to have? _____ (clue: how many cents are in a dollar?)

• **millipede**

Another insect that seems to have a thousand feet is a(n) _____.

• **pedal**

To make a car move faster, you press down on the gas _____.

• **pedestal**

A small statuette is often placed on a(n) _____. (foot stall; a base or foundation for a statue) If a man places a woman on a pedestal he treats her as though she were more godlike than human.

• **child leading**
  ped: child
  agogy: leading

Ped also can mean "child," so *pedagogy* literally means "_____." Pedagogy means the art or science of teaching.

• **pedophile**

Most grownups love children and treat them well. However, those who abuse them sexually are known as _____.

• **feet**

A *pediatrician* is one who treats children, whereas a *podiatrist* treats _____. For diseases affecting children, you would

• **pediatrician**
• **podiatrist**

go to see a(n) _____. For foot problems, you would go to see a(n) _____.

SELF-TEST

1. Their marriage faltered because John insisted on putting his wife on a pedestal, and she wanted to be treated normally. What is a pedestal? _____

2. Most people in education feel that physical punishment is not a necessary component of pedagogy. What is pedagogy? _____

3. The novel Iolita is about a middle-aged _____ , who falls in love with a twelve-year-old girl. (lover of children)

4. Dr. Lenny adored children, which helped make him a highly successful _____. (children's doctor)

5. Sheep, goats, and dogs are quadrupeds. Quadrupeds means
_____.

6. Man is a(n) _____. (two-legged creature)

1. the base on which a statue stands 2. art of teaching or "child-leading" 3. pedagogue
4. pediatrician 5. four-legged creatures 6. biped

20   POLIT, POLIS: city, citizen

Other Roots   **Suffixes**
acro: high   *an:* belonging to
cosmo: world   *ian:* one who
metro: mother   *ite:* a person associated with

Derivatives   Acropolis (uh KROP uh liss)
cosmopolitan (koz muh PAHL uh ton)
cosmopolite (koz MOP uh light)
Indianapolis (in dee un AP uh liss-
metropolis (muh TROP uh liss)
politician (pahl uh TISH un)

- **Indianapolis**

The city of the Indians is _____.

- **mother city**

The main city of a region is a metropolis. If *metro* means "mother,"
metropolis literally means _____.

- **high city**
  acro: high
  polis: city

In ancient Athens the highest part of the city, strongly fortified, was
known as the *Acropolis,* which means _____.

- **politician**

Every Greek citizen took an active part in the government of his city-
state. In current use only someone who is in some way active in politics
is called a(n) _____, and the word is often used to
mean a person who is active chiefly for his own gain or because he
enjoys power.

- **world citizen**
  cosmo: world
  polit: citizen

A *cosmopolite* is, literally, a "_____." A person who
feels at home in any part of the world is a *cosmopolite.* Her interests and
tastes are not narrowed to her own nation or country; they are interna-

- **cosmopolitan**

tional or _____. (belonging to a citizen of the world)

SELF-TEST

1. When John Fredericks returned from the goldfields, San Francisco had become a thriving _____. (main or mother city)

2. During the great age of seafaring, even small New England towns had about them a strongly cosmopolitan atmosphere. What does cosmopolitan mean here? _____

3. Our hotel room in Athens looked out toward the ruins of the Acropolis. The ruins were: on a river bank/on a hilltop/underground tunnels.

4. Although Ms. Mayberry had traveled widely during her career, she still retained a great many local and national prejudices, and she could not by any stretch of the imagination be called a(n) _____. (citizen of the world)

5. Indianapolis means "_____."

6. The House Majority Whip refers to himself as a "political leader"; I am inclined to think of him as just another _____. (a person active in politics)

ANSWERS

1. metropolis 2. international; reflecting all parts of the world 3. on a hilltop 4. cosmopolite 5. city of the Indians 6. politician

21   POLY: many

Other Roots	Suffixes
andr: husband, man	*ic:* marked by
graph: record	*y:* practice of
ling: tongue, language	
phone: sound (music)	
tech: trade, skill	

Derivatives   polyandry (pahl ee ANN dree)
polygraph (PAHL ee graff)
polylingual (pahl ee LING wuhl)
Polynesia (pahl uh NEEZ yuh)
polyphonic (pahl uh FAHN ik)
polysyllabic (pahl ee sil LAB ik)
polytechnic (pahl ee TEK nik)

- **it is made up of many syllables**

What is meant by saying that a word is *polysyllabic?*
_____

- **polylingual**

If you speak two languages, you are *bilingual*. If you speak more than two, you are _____.

- **polyandry**
  poly: many
  andr: husband

In some cultures a woman is allowed to have more than one husband at a time, a practice called _____ (many husbands). (Compare this term with *polygamy,* studied earlier, which is the practice of a person having more than one spouse. *Polyandry* and *polygamy* are the appropriate terms when the culture approves of or allows multiple marriages; *bigamy* is restricted to a multiple marriage that is against the law.)

- **many islands**

Nes means "island." The name Polynesia is given to a series of island groups scattered across the Pacific Ocean. *Polynesia* means

_____.

- **many trades or skills used in industry**

What would you expect to study at a *polytechnic* high school?
_____

- **polyphonic**

What do we call music that has two or more voice parts, each having an independent melody but all harmonizing? _____.
("many sounds")

- **polygraph**

Because a lie detector records tracings of several different pulsations at the same time, it is known officially as a(n) _____.
("many records")

SELF-TEST

1. The university choir specializes in singing polyphonic music. Polyphonic means _____.

2. To a beginning student of vocabulary, _____ words may seem difficult because they look like "big words." (marked by many syllables")

3. Sasha and Miljan lived in Greece with their British father and Serbian mother; by age three they were polylingual. Polylingual means

_____.

4. Until almost the twentieth century some of the valley tribes practiced polyandry, which is the practice of _____.

5. The vacant building may be refurbished and reopened as a(n) _____ high school. (offering instruction in many trades and skills)

6. Baker teaches the art of lie detection to policemen and security agents from around the world. He has made many refinements in the use of the _____. ("many records")

22 PROTO: first, fundamental

Other Roots	Suffixes
agon: struggle	*ist:* one who
plasm: something molded	
zoa: animals	

Derivatives   protagonist (pro TAG uh nist)
protocol (PRO tuh call)
protoplasm (PRO to plaz um)
prototype (PRO tuh type)
protozoa (pro tuh ZO uh)

• **prototype**   The first or primary *type* of anything is the _____.

• **protagonist**   The main character in a play (or the central figure in a contest or conflict) is the one with whom we fundamentally identify. He is the hero or _____. (one who is first in the struggle)

• **first animals**   Protozoa are one-celled creatures that belong to the most primitive section of the animal kingdom. If *zoa* means "animals," then *protozoa* means "_____."

• **protoplasm**   A watery or gelatinous substance considered the basis of physical life is called _____. (something molded first)

• **protocol**   If you have just received an appointment as an officer or as an ambassador, you will quickly have to learn a system of etiquette known as _____, which in a sense means knowing who comes first in military or diplomatic circles.

SELF-TEST   1. The modern airplane has its _____ in the paper gliders made and thrown by schoolchildren. (first model or pattern)

2. Protocol required that the retiring general be given first consideration. Protocol is _____.

3. Some form of _____ exists in almost every habitat, such as fresh or salt water, soil, sewage, and even the bodies of larger living animals. ("first animals")

4. In the movie "Schindler's List," the protagonist is an ambitious indus-
trialist who uses concentration camp inmates to run his factory and
saves them from the gas chambers. Protagonist means
_____.

5. Nourishment passes up through a plant from cell to cell, each of
which consists of single units of _____. (something
molded first; the substance that is the basis for all life)

1. prototype 2. a system of etiquette 3. protozoa 4. hero or main character; "first in
struggle" 5. protoplasm

23 PYR: fire

Other Roots	**Suffixes**
graph: writing	*iac:* one who
mania: madness	*y:* act of
phobia: fear	
technics: skill, craft	

Derivatives
pyre (PIRE)
Pyrex (PIE rex)
pyrography (pie ROG ruh fee)
pyromania (pie roe MAIN ee uh)
pyromaniac (pie roe MAIN ee ak)
pyrophobia (pie roe FOBE ee uh)
pyrotechnics (pie roe TEK niks)

- **pyrography**
  pyr: fire
  graph: writing
  y: act of

Burning designs on wood, leather, and so on is an art known as
_____.

- **a fire used to
  cremate a corpse**

In some cultures, when a husband died the widow was placed on the
funeral *pyre* and cremated along with him. What does *pyre* mean in
this context? _____

- **fire madness**
  pyr: fire
  mania: madness

Pyromania literally means _____.

• **pyromaniac**   A _____ has an irrational desire to set things on fire, unlike an arsonist, who sets a fire to get revenge or collect insurance money.

• **pyrotechnics**   The making or display of fireworks is called _____. ("fire crafts") The meaning is often extended to other areas. For example, a pianist's *pyrotechnics* would be his brilliant display of skill, especially in performing difficult music.

• **fear of fire**   A person who has *pyrophobia* suffers abnormally from _____.

SELF-TEST

1. A pyrophobe and a(n) _____ would make strange companions. (one with fire madness)

2. If we say that an opera singer is famous for her vocal pyrotechnics, what do we mean? _____

3. All of a warrior's most cherished belongings were placed near him on his funeral _____. (fire)

4. A morbid fear of fire is called _____.

5. Food cooked in a(n) _____ casserole dish requires a slightly lower oven temperature. (brand name for fireproof).

6. Having already mastered two difficult crafts, Jonathan decided to take a course in pyrography, which is the art of _____.

ANSWERS   1. pyromaniac 2. that she sings with technique as brilliant as fireworks 3. pyre 4. pyrophobia 5. Pyrex 6. burning designs on wood or leather

24   SCOP: see

Prefixes	Other Roots	Suffixes
epi: over	*horo:* hour	*al:* marked by
peri: around	*micro:* small	*y:* act of, science of
	stetho: chest	
	tele: far, distant	

Derivatives   episcopal (ee PISS kuh puhl)
horoscope (HORE uh scope)
microscope (MEYE kruh scope)
microscopy (meye KROSS kuh pee)

periscope (PEAR uh scope)
scope (SCOPE)
stethoscope (STETH uh scope)
telescope (TELL uh scope)

- **microscope**

- **microscopy**

Almost everyone knows that an instrument for seeing small things is a(n) _____, but few people know that the science of using microscopes is called _____.

- **see around**
  peri: around
  scope: see

A submarine commander sends up a *periscope* when he wishes to _____ the surface of the water.

- **telescope**
  tele: far
  scope: see

An instrument that helps man see far-off objects such as planets and stars is a(n) _____.

- **see the chest**

A *stethoscope* is literally an instrument used to _____, but in actuality it is used for hearing sounds in the chest.

- **scope**

The part of an area or problem that the examiners decide to deal with, or "see," is called the _____ of the examination.

- **horoscope**

A forecast that is supposed to "see" your future from the position of the stars at the *hour* of your birth is called your _____.

- **It is governed by overseers (bishops).**
  epi: over
  scop: see

What does the word *episcopal* tell you about the structure of the Episcopal Church? _____

SELF-TEST

1. In his study of viruses Dr. Danvers needs two assistants who are experts in tissue preparation and _____. (science of using microscopes)

2. During World War I, soldiers spent a great deal of time in deep trenches. To observe military activity above ground in safety, it was common practice to use a periscope, which allowed them to

   _____.

3. The comet was visible only through a very powerful _____.

4. Mrs. Doolittle would not sign the contract because her horoscope warned against business activities on Tuesday. A horoscope is

   _____.

5. The special prosecutor told reporters she was expanding the
_____ of her investigation. (area to be seen)

6. Which church takes its name from the fact that it is governed by
bishops?

1. microscopy 2. see around 3. telescope 4. a forecast based on star positions at the hour
of birth 5. scope 6. Episcopal Church

25   THE: god

Prefixes	Other Roots	Suffixes
apo: change	*cracy:* rule by	*ic:* marked by
mono: one	*logy:* study of	*ism:* belief in
poly: many		*osis:* process

Derivatives
apotheosis (uh POTH ee uh sis)
apotheosize (uh POTH ee uh size)
atheism (AY thee izm)
monotheism (MON oh thee izm)
polytheism (PAHL ee thee izm)
theism (THEE izm)
theocracy (thee OK ruh see)
theocratic (thee uh KRAT ik)
theology (thee AHL uh gee)

- **theism**
the: god
ism: belief in

Belief in the existence of a god is called _____.

- **a belief in the existence of one god**

Monotheism is _____.

- **a belief in the existence of many gods**

Polytheism is _____.

- **without a belief in the existence of a god or gods**

Atheism is being _____.

• **theology**	The study of the nature of God and of god's relations to humankind and the universe is called _____.
• **god**	To *apotheosize* an athlete or a hero or a politician is to treat her as though she were a(n) _____.
• **apotheosis**	The process of raising a human being to the status of a god is called _____.
• **rule by god**	*Theocracy* means literally "_____." The religious leaders and the political leaders were closely connected, and were sometimes the same people, in the early Puritan colonies in New England.
• **theocratic**	These colonies had a(n) _____ system of government.

SELF-TEST

1. In associating _____ with primitive people, he overlooked the Greeks and Romans, who were highly sophisticated yet prayed to many gods. (belief in many gods)

2. Some foreign observers point out that we Americans give our favorite athletes an uncritical adoration and reverence that amounts almost to apotheosis. What is apotheosis? _____

3. Most of the American colonies founded by religious groups tended to have a theocratic structure, at least in their formative years. Theocratic structure means _____.

4. Fans appeared to be trying to _____ the quarterback, until he was arrested. (make into a god)

5. Both Judaism and Christianity are based on _____. (belief in one god)

6. My two uncles continually argue about women, politics, and _____. (study of the existence and nature of God)

ANSWERS   1. polytheism 2. process of raising a man or woman to a god 3. "rule by god," with religious and political leaders much the same 4. apotheosize 5. monotheism 6. theology

Now that you've mastered this chapter, you might enjoy a fresh look at the drawing that opens it on page 10.

HYPERTOASTER

CATACONE

HYPOACTIVE

SYNKIN

3   Greek Prefixes

1   A-, AN-: without

Roots	**Suffixes**
arch: chief or ruler of government	*al:* relating to
	ia: condition
byss: bottom	*ism:* condition
damant: subdued	*ist:* one who
em: blood	*ize:* verb ending
esthet: sensation	*y:* state of
odyne: pain	
path: feeling	
the: god	

Derivatives

abyss (uh BISS)
adamant (AD uh munt)
amoral (ay MOR uhl)
anarchist (AN er kist)
anarchy (AN er kee)
anemia (uh NEEM ee uh)
anemic (uh NEEM ik)
anesthetize (uh NEZ thuh tize)
anodyne (AN uh dine)

apathetic (ap uh THET ik)
asymmetrical (ay sim MET ree kuhl)
atheism (AY thee izm)
atheist (AY thee ist)
atypical (ay TIP uh kuhl)

• **a**	In the previous chapter you learned that an atheist is a person without a belief in God. The word is formed by adding the prefix _____ to *theist*. If *theism* means having a belief in God,
• **atheism**	then the word meaning without a belief in God is _____.
• **not pay**	*Damant* means "being subdued." To be *adamant* means to be stubbornly opposed to or insistent upon something. If you are *adamant* that you have been overcharged at a store, are you likely to pay your bill or not?
• **without feeling**	To be apathetic about the fate of other human beings is to be: without feeling/deeply concerned. Even if you did not recall from an earlier unit that path means "feeling," you could have chosen the right answer by
• **without**	knowing that *a-* means _____.
• **asymmetrical**	If the left and right sides of a human face are without balance, then it is a(n) _____ face. (not symmetrical)
• **atypical**	To behave in typical fashion is to behave as most other people would in a given circumstance. Thousands of children laugh at the pranks of a clown; the one child that cries is *atypical*. Whether it is a rock sample or a statistic, something that lies outside (without) the expected pattern is _____.
• **amoral**	An act that is "not moral" is immoral. But if an act is committed without regard for the concept of right and wrong, it is _____.
• **without pain** *an:* without *odyne:* pain	The prefix *an-* also means "without." It is a form of *a-* used before roots beginning with a vowel. Thus, *anodyne* literally means _____. The medical term for pain relievers is anodynes.
• **without blood** *an:* without *em:* blood • **anemic**	The term *anemia* literally means _____. Anemia normally means a person's blood is lacking in some way. In more general usage, a person who has no "life" or vitality is said to be _____.

- **so that he will feel no sensation of pain**
  an: without
  esthet: sensation

Why is a patient *anesthetized* before an operation? _____.

- **without rule or government**
- **anarchist**

Anarchy means _____. Thus a person who engages in destructive acts against a government to bring it down, to be without a government, is called a(n) _____.

- **a bottomless hole**

During an exploration of the North Pole, two scientists were lost when their sled fell into an abyss. What is an *abyss?* _____

- **abyss**

The pit of hell is sometimes referred to as "the _____." (bottomless pit) More commonly, the word is used in a metaphorical sense to emphasize or even exaggerate our feelings. In a fit of despair Margaret says she feels she is standing on the edge of an *abyss*. She means that she may fall into: a short period of illness/an immeasurably hopeless or wretched condition.

- **an immeasurably hopeless or wretched condition**

SELF-TEST

1. A blood test reveals that Mary suffers from a mild _____. (lack in the blood)

2. After the _____ wore off, the patient woke up and groaned.

3. The professor dismissed John's example of prejudice as being uncharacteristic and therefore _____. (outside the expected pattern)

4. The governor was *adamant* in her stand against the proposed legislation. The governor was: angry/incorrect/firm.

5. After the Federal Reserve raised interest rates, the president said the country had moved to the brink of an economic abyss. Abyss means _____.

6. The actress preferred to be photographed from her left side because her _____ face looked better from that side. (without symmetry)

7. Believing in neither right nor wrong, Hubert felt his acts could only be considered amoral, not immoral. *Amoral* means _____.

8. The tiny kingdom was threatened from the outside by a powerful army; from the inside, by increasing signs of _____. (state of being without a government; chaos in government)

9. With the exponential rise of government budget deficits, middle-class taxpayers have become increasingly *apathetic* toward the plight of the poor. That is, they seem to be _____.

10. A person who doesn't believe in God is a(n) _____.

2   ANTI-, ANT-: against

Roots	Suffixes
agon: struggle	*al:* relating to
bio: life	*ic:* relating to
dote: poison	*ist:* one who
path: feeling	*y:* state of

Derivatives

antibiotic (an tee beye AHT ik)
anticlimax (an tee KLEYE max)
antidote (AN tee dote)
antipathy (an TIP uh thee)
antiseptic (an tee SEP tik)
antisocial (an tee SO shuhl)
antitrust (an tee TRUST)
anti-American (an tee American)
anti-Christian (an tee Christian)
antagonist (an TAG uh nist)
Antarctic (ant ARK tik)
antagonize

- **anti**
- **against**
- **against**

Study these words carefully: *antiwar, anti-aircraft*. Both begin with the prefix _____. If you are antiwar, you are _____ war; anti-aircraft guns are used _____ aircraft.

- **antisocial**

If a person dislikes social occasions such as parties and does not seem to desire companionship, she is probably _____. ("against social")

- **antibiotic**
  anti: against
  bio: life

At some time or other almost everyone has taken a pill or had an injection that helps fight an infection. A medicine that fights "living" bacteria is commonly known as a(n) _____.

• **against poison** *anti:* against *dote:* poison	An *antidote* is a substance that works _____. The meaning can be extended to mean a remedy for any kind of evil.
• **antiseptic**	A *septic* condition involves bacteria and decay. To prevent or retard the growth of bacteria, we can use a(n) _____.
• **against**	*Sympathy* is a feeling together with someone; *antipathy* is a feeling _____ someone.
• **antipathy**	People we like call forth our sympathy at almost any time. People we strongly dislike bring forth our _____.
• **antitrust**	Legislatures often pass laws to protect the general public from large corporations or "trusts" that may attempt to corner the market on a product or discourage competition. Such laws are called _____ laws. (against trusts)
• **anticlimax**	The *climax* of a play, movie, or real-life drama like a war occurs when the central conflict is resolved. Usually this is also the highest point of interest—for example, when the hero unmasks the villain or defeats him. If the drama continues on to a less-interesting event, then that event is called a(n) _____. ("against climax")
• **anti-Christian**	In the word *anti-American* the prefix is used with a hyphen because it is joined to a proper noun, which is of course capitalized. Write down the word you would form to mean "against that which is Christian." _____
• **Antarctic**	The variant prefix *ant-* is sometimes used before roots beginning with a vowel (*antacid* = ant + acid). If the Arctic is located at the top of the Northern Hemisphere, what do we call the similar region located opposite it, in the Southern Hemisphere? The _____.
• **antagonists** *agon:* struggle *ist:* one who	Two people who fight against each other are opponents or _____.
• **it angers you (and you oppose her)**	If a friend's remark *antagonizes* you, what does it do? _____
	In the discussion of plays you will often encounter the terms *protagonist* and *antagonist*. They are a carryover from Greek athletic contests. The *protagonist* is the champion we are rooting for; the *antagonist* is

the one who opposes him. Thus in a play the *protagonist* is the hero and the *antagonist* is the villain.

1. The dentist recommended that she gargle with a mouthwash containing a mild _____. (a substance that helps prevent decay)

2. Because the enemy soldiers hardly put up any resistance, the war turned out to be an anticlimax compared with the preparation. An *anticlimax* is _____.

3. The two former friends, now _____, are doing their best to discredit each other politically. (opponents)

4. Janet's shaming laughter and her refusal to listen to his explanation produced in Fred a deep and unexpected antipathy. *Antipathy* means _____.

5. Charlotte's easy acceptance of him was a(n) _____ for the poisonous self-doubts that had crept into his mind. (remedy for an evil)

6. From Dick's behavior at the party it was difficult to tell whether he was _____ or just too tired to relate to anyone. ("against social")

7. Her fever began to go down a few hours after she took the antibiotic. What is an *antibiotic?* _____

1. antiseptic 2. "against climax" or a descent from the important to the trivial 3. antagonists 4. dislike; feeling against 5. antidote 6. antisocial 7. a medicine against infection or virus

3 CATA-: down

Roots	Suffixes
act: dash	*ic:* relating to
clys: wash	
log: reasoning	
lyst: break	
pult: hurl	
strophe: turn	

Derivatives   cataclysm (KAT uh klizm)
cataclysmic (kat uh KLIZ mik)
catacomb (KAT uh comb)

catalog (KAT uh log)
catalyst (KAT uh list)
catapult (KAT uh puhlt)
cataract (KAT uh rakt)
catastrophe (kuh TASST ruh fee)

• **to list and briefly describe them**	To shop from a mail order company, you look at its *catalog,* in which the items are "spoken down"—that is, written down or listed. *Catalog* can also be used as a verb. What would be your task if you were to *catalog* the paintings of a famous artist? _____
• **underground**	The early Christians hid from the Romans in the *catacombs,* or galleries containing burial vaults. The prefix helps you to determine that the catacombs were: aboveground/underground galleries.
• **cataclysm**	A violent storm causing great destruction is called a(n) _____. ("wash down") Such a storm lets loose tremendous quantities of water that "wash down" the countryside, changing the face of the land. Even though they do not involve water, other violent upheavals of nature, such as earthquakes, can also be
• **cataclysmic**	called _____ occurrences.
• **quickly**	In ancient times a machine used to hurl rocks against a wall or fortification was called a *catapult* ("down hurler"). A rock that was being catapulted would rise steeply into the air, trace an arc, and then fall downward. Today *catapult* is most often used as a verb, retaining chiefly the idea of something shooting upward at great speed. If a singer is catapulted into fame, he reaches fame very: quickly/slowly. This exemplifies how a word can gradually change, sometimes distorting, even reversing, its original meaning.
• **catastrophe**	In a play or in real life, when a man's fortunes suddenly and dramatically undergo a complete "downturn," we say he has suffered a(n) _____.
• **cataracts**	A *cataract* is the "dashing down" of water, as in a large waterfall. Steep rapids in a river and sudden torrents of rain can also be called _____ because in both cases there is a heavy
• **dashing down**	"_____" or downpouring of water. A *cataract* can
• **dashes down**	also be a cloudiness of the eye that "_____" over the lens, blotting vision.

• break down

A *catalyst* is "that which breaks (things) down." A *catalyst* triggers a chemical reaction without itself being changed. When it is added to two other substances, it causes them to "_____" and react with each other.

SELF-TEST

1. The sudden and dramatic drop in the stock market was a(n) _____ for many small investors. ("downturn")

2. Cataracts of rain quickly flooded the busy intersection. In this context *cataracts* are _____.

3. The flood of 1933 was the state's worst _____. (a violent storm causing great destruction)

4. Senator Johnson was *catapulted* into prominence when she published a book outlining the need for a third political party. How soon did she reach prominence? _____

5. If you were camping outdoors and the weatherman had predicted a storm of *cataclysmic* proportions, why would you be worried?
_____

6. To escape the pursuing Romans, Rubus and his family hid in the _____. (underground galleries containing burial vaults)

7. The sodium chloride was a simple _____ that allowed the other two substances to interact freely. ("that which breaks down")

ANSWERS

1. catastrophe 2. heavy downpours 3. cataclysm 4. very quickly 5. because the storm would be violent and destructive 6. catacombs 7. catalyst

4   DIA-: across, through, thoroughly

Roots	Suffixes
gnose: know	*al:* marked by
gon: corner	*ous:* marked by
log: speech	*y:* process
meter: measure	
phan: clear	
phragm: fenced	
rrhea: flow	
therm: heat	

Derivatives   diadem (DEYE uh dem)
diagnose (DEYE ugh nose)

diagonal (deye AG uh nuhl)
dialog (DEYE uh log)
diameter (deye AM uh tur)
diaphanous (deye AFF uh nuss)
diaphragm (DEYE uh fram)
diarrhea (deye uh RHEE uh)
diathermy (DEYE uh therm ee)

- **diagonal**
  dia: across
  gon: corner

If *gon* means "corner," what kind of line is drawn across a square from one corner to the opposite corner? A(n) _____ line.

- **across measure**
  dia: across
  meter: measure

If *meter* means "measure," *diameter* literally means "_____." In a circle, the diameter is a straight line passing from one side to the other giving the measure across the circle.

- **dialog**

If *log* means "words about" or "speech," what do we call a discussion between two people, as in a play? _____

- **know thoroughly**
  dia: thoroughly
  gnose: know

A doctor examines symptoms carefully to *diagnose* an illness. This current meaning is implied in the original meaning of *diagnose*, "to _____."

- **diarrhea**

What term is applied to an excessive discharge from the intestines ("a flowing through")? _____

- **diaphragm**

What term means "fenced across" and denotes a partition separating the chest from the abdominal cavities? _____

- *dia:* across

In early days a king wore a headband called a *diadem*. What part of the word *diadem* tells you it was worn bound about or across the head? _____

- **through**
  dia: through

A dress made of *diaphanous* material would be so fine-textured or sheer that it would permit seeing _____.

SELF-TEST

1. A heating pad is one simple device for administering _____. (heat through)

2. A new bride might prefer to wear a nightgown that is nearly *diaphanous*, which is: made of beads/a "see-through" gown/wash and wear.

3. Diarrhea often causes dehydration because fluids _____ the patient.

4. Singers practice breathing exercises to strengthen the muscles of the _____. (a body partition separating the chest from the abdominal cavities)

5. The editor drew a *diagonal* line across the page that was to be omitted from the manuscript. How was the line drawn on the page?

_____

6. Albert was examined by four specialists before one of them was able to _____ his ailment. ("know thoroughly")

1. diathermy 2. a "see-through" gown 3. flow through 4. diaphragm 5. across the page from corner to corner 6. diagnose

5 EPI-: on, upon

Roots
dermis: skin
gram: writing
lepsy: take or seize
logue: speech
taph: tomb
thet: put
tome: cut short

Suffixes
ize: verb ending

Derivatives
epidermis (ep uh DERM iss)
epigram (EP uh gram)
epilepsy (EP uh lep see)
epilogue (EP uh log)
epitaph (EP uh taff)
epithet (EP uh thet)
epitome (ee PIT uh mee)
epitomize (ee PIT uh mize)

• **on the skin**
  epi: on
  dermis: skin

Epidermis, which means _____, is actually the outermost layer of skin.

• **epilepsy**

A nervous disorder in which the victim is seized or taken *on* by fits is called _____.

• **epigram**	An *epigram* is a brief, witty comment on a single subject. For example, "All animals are created equal, but some are more equal than others," is a(n) _____.
• **"on put" or put on** *epi:* on *thet:* put	*Thet* means "put," so *epithet* means _____. If you hurl *epithets* at someone, you put abusive names on him (racist, sissy, bleeding heart).
• **speech on** *epi:* on *logue:* speech	A play or book may begin with a prologue (a "speech before") and end with an *epilogue*, which is literally a(n) _____. The epilogue is a final speech or commentary on what happened earlier.
• **on or upon a tomb-stone**	The word *epitaph* breaks down into *epi-* + *taph* (tomb) and means the inscription where? _____. In one sense the word *epitomize* breaks down into *epi-* + *tomize* ("to cut short") and means to summarize briefly what was most typical or ideal. "Here lies John Thompson—kind husband, loving father, good citizen." You
• **epitomize** • **epitaph**	might _____ someone's life by composing a(n) _____ for her tombstone.
• **to summarize or embody**	Bob's experience *epitomizes* what happens to a freshman in a large university. Here *epitomize* means to summarize or embody/to be one among many.
• **an ideal representa-tion of patience**	If Ms. Jones is the *epitome* of patience, she is: an ideal representation of patience/a bad example of patience.

SELF-TEST

1. Bureaucrat, career politician, reactionary, socialist, and draft dodger are used as epithets by people of different political points of view. An epithet is _____.

2. His _____ read simply, "He loved God and his fellow man." (tombstone inscription)

3. In the epilogue of the play the father states that he never really understood his two sons. The *epilogue* comes: before the play/between the acts/at the end of the play.

4. Oscar Wilde called fox hunting, "The unspeakable in pursuit of the inedible." This is a(n) _____.(a short, witty remark)

5. Ms. Carruthers epitomized everything Sue liked in a boss. *Epitomized* means _____.

6. Man is still a creature of the sea, able to leave it only because, from birth to death, he lives in the water-filled spacesuit formed by his _____. (outermost layer of skin)

1. an abusive name "put on" someone 2. epitaph 3. at the end of the play 4. epigram 5. summarized the typical or ideal 6. epidermis

6 EC-: out, outside

Roots
centr: center
clesi: clergy
lect: pick, choose
lipse: omit, blot
mast: breast
morph: form
stas: put
tom: cut
zema: boil

Suffixes
ic, ical: relating to, marked by
ically: adverb ending
ity, y: act of, state of, property of

Derivatives

appendectomy (appen DECK tuh mee)
eccentric (ek SEN trik)
eccentricity (ek sen TRISS uh tee)
ecclesiastic (ik kleez ee ASS tik)
ecclesiastical (ik kleez ee ASS tuh kuhl)
eclectic (ik LEK tik)
eclipse (ee KLIPS)
ecstasy (EK stuh see)
ecstatic (ek STAT ik)
ecstatically (ek STAT ik lee)
ectomorphic (ek toe MORF ik)
ectopic (ek TOP ik)
eczema (EK zuh muh)
mastectomy (mass TEK tuh mee)
tonsillectomy (tahn sill LEK tuh mee)

• **eczema**
 ec: out
 zema: boil

If *zema* means "boil," which derivative describes a condition in which sores seem to boil out of the skin? _____

• **He blotted out her importance.**

When the moon passes between the earth and the sun and blots out the sun, we call the event an *eclipse*. What does *eclipse* mean when used as a verb, in this sentence? Jonathan easily eclipsed his sister as an entertainer. _____

- **no**

Professor Barnes has an *eclectic* taste in music. If *lect* means "choose," does she like only one kind of music—say, classical? _____ You answered correctly if you figured that eclectic taste is based on selecting, or picking out, from many different choices.

- **ecclesiastic**

- **the church or the clergy**

Originally *ecclesi* meant "to call forth (out)" and then came to mean an assembly of citizens or church. Today a clergyman or preacher can be called a(n) _____, and when we speak of *ecclesiastical* affairs, we mean affairs that pertain to _____.

- **outside**

"Eccentric Leaves Millions to Cat." Why would this headline be of interest? Because it describes someone doing something very unusual or odd. *Eccentric* actions are _____ customary human behavior. Most of us have at least one little oddity or

- **eccentricity**

_____.

- **outside**

Have you ever heard the expression "Beside himself with joy"? The derivative naming this high emotional state is ecstasy, which means standing _____ oneself. When he received the

- **ecstatic**

award, Mike was _____. (adjective form)

- **ecstatically**

When Martha received the necklace, she sighed _____. (adverb form)

- **appendectomy**
- **tonsillectomy**
- **mastectomy**

Many medical terms end in *-ectomy* ("act of cutting out"). Removal of an appendix = _____; of tonsils = _____; of a breast ("mast") = _____.

SELF-TEST

1. Reverend Trumbull has accepted an invitation to be a featured speaker at an *ecclesiastical* conference in Midland. The conference will be attended by: religious leaders/athletic coaches/businessmen.

2. In the poem John tried to capture the _____ of his love for Mary. (high emotional state)

3. The cook thought I was _____ because I asked to have my fried eggs chilled in the refrigerator before they were served. (odd or very unusual)

4. His extensive collection of books—light and serious, ancient and modern, classical and popular, American and European—proved that his taste in reading was eclectic. *Eclectic* means _____.

5. The skin eruptions are possibly an indication of
_____. ("boil out")

6. Selma recovered from the mastectomy much quicker than she thought possible. A *mastectomy* is _____.

ANSWERS   1. religious leaders 2. ecstasy 3. eccentric 4. based on selecting the best from many sources 5. eczema 6. removal of a breast

7   EU-: good, pleasant

Roots	Suffixes
gen: race	*ia:* act of
logy: speech	*ic:* marked by
peps: stomach	*ically:* adverb ending
phem: statement	*ism:* property of
(speech)	*ize:* verb ending
phon: sound	*ous:* marked by
phor: bring	*y:* property of
thanas: death	

Derivatives

eugenics (yoo GEN iks)
eulogize (YOOL uh gize)
eulogy (YOOL uh gee)
eupepsia (yoo PEP see uh)
euphemism (YOOF uh mizm)
euphemistically (yoof uh MIST ik lee)
euphonious (yoo PHONE ee us)
euphony (YOO fun ee)
euphoria (yoo FORE ee uh)
euphoric (yoo FORE ik)
euthanasia (yoo thuh NAY zhuh)

• **He is praised; good things are said about him.**
eu: pleasant
log: speech

One of the meanings of *logos* is "speech." If a man is *eulogized* at his funeral, what do we mean? _____

• **good or pleasant**

Dr. Kevorkian promotes *mercy killing* for those who are suffering greatly during a terminal illness. This is called *euthanasia,* which literally means "_____ death."

- **euphonious**
  eu: pleasant
  phon: sound
  ious: marked by

If *phon* means "sound," what kind of voice produces pleasant or melodious sounds? a(n) _____ voice.

- **eugenics**

Which derivative denotes the science of improving the genetic characteristics of the human race? _____

- **good or pleasant**

When a large company is preparing to lay off large numbers of employees, management prefers to speak of "downsizing" or "rightsizing" because it sounds better than "firing." They are using a euphemism—a(n) _____ term instead of a harsh one.

- **euphemistically**

Sometimes you might prefer that someone would talk to you honestly rather than _____.

- **pleasantness, well-being**
- **euphoric**

The prefix *eu-* indicates that *euphoria* is an intense and sometimes abnormal feeling of _____. Some people drink or resort to drugs to bring on a(n) _____ state. (marked by a feeling of well-being)

- **eupepsia**

If dyspepsia is bad digestion, which derivative indicates good digestion? _____

SELF-TEST

1. The little band of pioneers huddled together in the cold while the parson delivered a brief _____ over Buck's grave. (praising speech)

2. The parson hurried over Buck's hard drinking by referring to it _____ as "Buck's one little weakness." (using a pleasant statement rather than a harsh one)

3. If a doctor withdraws life-support systems from an incurably ill person in terrible pain, that act is called _____.

4. The medicine given him by the native guide not only took away the pain, but also brought on an otherwise unexplainable _____. (exaggerated feeling of well-being)

5. The young actress thought that Marilyn Monroe was a more *euphonious* name than Norma Jean Baker. That is, "Marilyn Monroe" sounded more _____.

6. Hitler readily embraced eugenics as a means of creating a German superrace. *Eugenics* is the pseudo-science of _____.

HYPER-: over, excessive
HYPO-: under, less than

Roots

bol: throw
chondr: breastplate
derm: skin
glycem: sugar
therm: heat
thes: put

Suffixes

ia: condition
iac: one who
is: noun ending
ism: condition

Derivatives

hyperactive (heye per AK tive)
hyperbole (heye PERB uh lee)
hypercritical (heye per KRIT uh kuhl)
hypersensitive (heye per SENZ uh tiv)
hyperthermia (heye per THERM ee uh)
hyperthyroidism (heye per THEYE roid izm)
hypoactive (heye poe AK tive)
hypochondriac (heye poe KOND ree ak)
hypodermic (heye poe DERM ik)
hypoglycemia (heye poe glie SEEM ee uh)
hypothermia (heye poe THERM ee uh)
hypothesis (heye POTH uh sis)
hypothetical (heye poe THET uh kuhl)
hypothyroidism (heye poe THEYE roid izm)

- **hypersensitive**
  hyper: over

An excessively sensitive person is _____.

- **overactive; abnormally restless and fidgety**

A *hyperactive* child is _____.

- **hypercritical**

John criticizes his wife's clothing very severely. She probably thinks of him as being _____.

- **hyperbole**

Hyperbole is an extreme statement made for effect. "Your heart is as cold as ice!" is an example of _____.

- **under**
  hypo: under
  derm: skin

- **An injection cannot be given *over the skin*.**

If *derm* means "skin," a *hypodermic* needle gives an injection _____ the skin. Perhaps you have heard someone say "hyperdermic" needle. Why is "hyperdermic" incorrect? _____

- **hypothyroidism**

- **hyperthyroidism**

Hyper- and *hypo-* are used to describe many medical conditions. An insufficient production of thyroxin is _____; an excessive production of thyroxin is _____.

- **hyperthermia**
- **hypothermia**

Above-normal body temperature would be _____; below-normal temperature is _____.

- **under**

- **made up but having the appearance of truth**

Charles Darwin's hypothesis was that only the fittest of the species survive. Here *hypothesis* means an explanation placed _____ the facts and thought likely to be a true explanation. (Like a *theory*, a *hypothesis* is an explanation that is not yet proved, merely assumed.) If in arguing someone cites a *hypothetical* example, he is using an illustration that is: real/made up but having the appearance of truth.

- **hypochondriac**

The ancient Greeks thought that melancholy was located under the cartilage of the breastplate (*hypo + chondros*). A person in physical or emotional pain was supposed to clutch his breastplate—or at least actors portrayed them as doing so. Today a person who suffers from imaginary ailments, who in effect clutches his breastplate too often and without genuine cause, is called a(n) _____.

SELF-TEST

1. To be *hypoactive* is to be _____.

2. "My love is as deep as the ocean" is an example of *hyperbole*, which is _____.

3. Because I reported in to sick bay three times in two weeks, the captain branded me as a *hypochondriac*. That is, he thought I was _____.

4. The doctor said the antibiotic could be given only in a(n) _____ injection. (under the skin)

5. To disguise the identities of the two informants, the detective used a(n) _____ example to describe the evidence. (made up but having the appearance of truth)

6. A condition in which the body temperature is below normal is _____.

9   PARA-, PAR-: alongside

Roots	Suffixes
allel: of one another	*al:* relating to
ble (bol): throw	*ia:* things
noia: mind	
oide: song	
phernal: dowry	
phrase: say	
sitos: food	

Derivatives   parable (PEAR uh buhl)
parallel (PEAR uh lell)
paranoia (pear uh NOY yuh)
paraphernalia (pear uh fer NAIL yuh)
paraphrase (PEAR uh fraze)
paraprofessional (pear uh pro FESS shun uhl)
parasite (PEAR uh site)
parody (PEAR uh dee)

- **alongside**
  para: alongside

  Parallel lines run _____ each other and are everywhere equidistant from each other.

- **alongside**

  A *parasite* lives beside and feeds on another plant or animal. Literally *parasite* breaks down into *para* (_____) + *sitos* (food). In anger, what might you call a sponging relative who makes no

- **a parasite**

  effort to support himself? _____

- **paraphrase**

  Phrase means "say." If you cannot remember a quotation exactly, then you say it in your own words, or _____ it. ("say alongside")

- **parody**

  If *par* means "alongside" and *oide* means "song," which of the derivatives would describe a nonsensical imitation of a serious piece of writing? _____

  Today we say that someone with a mental derangement is out of her mind. The Greek word for madness was *paranoia*—a state of being alongside one's mind.

• **para** Which part of the word means "alongside"? _____
It is worth noting that the person suffering from *paranoia* usually has delusions of being persecuted or else has delusions of importance.

• **alongside a professional** A *paraprofessional* is someone who works _____.
A paraprofessional usually performs some professional duties under the supervision of a qualified professional, such as a doctor or teacher.

• **alongside** Jesus often taught the multitudes by using *parables*. The word *parable* originally meant a comparison, and derives from para ("_____") + *ble* ("thrown"). A *parable* is a brief story that illustrates a moral or spiritual truth.

• **alongside** *Paraphernalia* originally meant "_____ the dowry" and was applied to the personal belongings a bride took along with her. Paraphernalia still means personal belongings, but more specifically it means equipment or materials for a special purpose. Thus, in packing for a camping trip, you would include a backpack, a tent, and other

• **paraphernalia** _____. (equipment brought along)

SELF-TEST

1. The tree was slowly being destroyed by two different parasites. What is a *parasite*? _____

2. The store was closed for selling drug _____. (equipment associated with a particular activity)

3. The movie audience laughed uproariously at the parody of "Top Gun" called "Hot Shots." What is a parody? _____

4. The kindergarten class would have been even more chaotic if there had been no _____ to help the teacher. (someone who works alongside a professional)

5. Betty's grandfather had no doubt intended the story to be a(n) _____, but we failed to find a moral in it. (a story illustrating a moral)

6. His distrust and suspicion of everyone around him led us to believe that he was suffering from _____. (a madness characterized by delusions of persecution)

7. I could not recall the quotation exactly so I had to _____ it.

ANSWERS 1. something feeding on another plant or animal 2. paraphernalia 3. a comic imitation of serious writing 4. paraprofessional 5. parable 6. paranoia 7. paraphrase

10

PERI-: around, near

Roots	Suffixes
card: heart	*al:* relating to
gee: earth	*ic:* marked by
meter: measure	*ium:* that which
patet: walk	*y:* act of, result of
pher: carry	
scope: look	

Derivatives pericardium (pear uh KARD ee um)
perigee (PEAR uh gee)
perimeter (puh RIM uh ter)
peripatetic (pear uh puh TET ik)
peripheral (per IF er uhl)
periphery (per IF er ee)
periscope (PEAR uh skope)

- **look around**
peri: around
scope: look

A *periscope* is an instrument used in a submarine to _____ the surface of the ocean.

- **perimeter**
peri: around
meter: measure

If you walk all the way around the top of a volcano, you trace its outer measurement or _____.

- **peri**

Someone who is shy may wish to remain at the outer edge of a crowd; he feels more secure on the periphery. What part of the word *periphery* tells us the person is *around* the edge of the crowd? _____

- **she missed the main issues**

Why would you feel dissatisfied if a speaker had touched only on *peripheral* issues of a controversy? Because _____.

- **perigee**

Peri- can also mean "near." As the moon or a satellite revolves about the earth, it traces an oval rather than a completely round pattern. When the moon is farthest from earth, it is at its *apogee;* when nearest the earth, it is at its _____.

- **a peripatetic teacher**

Aristotle was known as the *peripatetic* philosopher because he liked to walk around from place to place as he philosophized. What would you call a teacher who paced the floor incessantly while talking to a class?

_____

• **around the heart** If card means "heart," where is the membranous sac called the *pericardium* located? _____

1. The _____ of the pond was nearly two thousand feet. ("measure around")

2. Dr. Murray's ideas are original and interesting, but I am frequently distracted by his peripatetic manner in front of an audience. *Peripatetic* means _____.

3. The committee members were in such disagreement they could decide only on _____ matters like printing some posters. (around the edge)

4. At its *perigee,* the satellite will be visible to the naked eye because at that time it will be only 157 miles from the earth. The *perigee* is its: nearest point/farthest point.

ANSWERS   1. perimeter 2. walking around 3. peripheral 4. nearest point

11 SYN-, SYM-, SYL-, SYS-: together, with

Roots   **Suffixes**
chron: time   *ism:* act of
lable: gather, take   *ium:* act of
log: reasoning   *ize:* verb ending
onym: name   *sis:* act of, process
op: eye   *y:* act of
path: feeling
pos: drink
tax: arrange
tem: to cause to stand
thes: put

Derivatives   syllable (SILL uh buhl)
                   syllogism (SILL uh jizm)
                   sympathy (SIM puh thee)
                   symposium (sim POSE ee um)
                   synchronize (SIN krun ize)
                   synonym (SIN uh nim)
                   synopsis (sin OP sis)
                   syntax (SIN tax)

synthesis (SIN thuh sis)
system (SIS tum)

- synonyms

The prefix *syn-* and its variants occur in many words that you already know. Words that mean approximately the same thing and can be used to define each other (for example, the words *hurtful* and *injurious*) are called _____. If you "feel with" another person

- sympathy

who is having troubles, you project _____ for that person. Letters are "gathered together" to form a sound called

- syllable

a(n) _____. Things are "caused to stand together"

- system

to form a(n) _____.

Because *synonym, sympathy, syllable,* and *system* are everyday words, you probably don't even think about the fact that you were using a different form for each one. The correct form is largely determined by what will sound best. Try saying "synlable," "symlable," or "syslable" and you will hear for yourself why the various forms exist.

- synchronize
  syn: together
  chron: time

Use the prefix *syn-* to complete the following sentence: The sergeant told his men to set their watches at the exact same time before they began their operation. That is, the sergeant told them to _____ their watches.

- together

You are warned to watch your *syntax;* you are to be careful how you arrange words _____ to form a sentence, phrase, or clause.

- view together
  syn: together
  op: view

An essay of five thousand words has been reduced to a one-paragraph *synopsis.* Literally, you are then able to _____ its main ideas.

- a short summary

A good synonym for synopsis would thus be: a light sketch/a short summary.

- getting together to exchange ideas

Originally *symposium* meant "drinking together." Here is an example of more current usage: Local police officers will attend a two-day symposium on riot control. What does *symposium* mean here?

_____

- syllogism

Here is a pattern of logic or reasoning commonly in use:
    All mortals must die.
    John is mortal.
    Therefore, John must die.

If the first two statements (called premises) are true, then the third statement (the conclusion) must also be true. This way of putting together ideas to arrive at a conclusion based on them is called a(n) _____. ("reasoning together")

Now look at this pattern:
    All lawyers are greedy.
    Clarence is a lawyer.
    Clarence is greedy.

• **syllogism**

Right? No—wrong! The _____ contains a faulty premise, because it remains to be proved that all lawyers are greedy.

• **together**

An analysis involves taking something apart into its separate, smaller units. A *synthesis* involves putting things _____ into a meaningful whole. You would make an analysis of a difficult essay to understand it better. On the other hand, your philosophy of life is probably a(n) _____ of concepts you have gleaned from a wide variety of people, influences, and experiences.

• **synthesis**

SELF-TEST

1. The new remedial English course will cover syntax and basic composition. What is *syntax*? _____

2. Your _____ is incorrect because in your major premise you assume that all neurotics have creative ability. (pattern of logic, with premises and conclusion)

3. Mr. Markov's theory of personality is a(n) _____ of psychological ideas taken from Freud, Jung, Horney, and Sullivan. (putting together)

4. The symposium on social planning is open to the public. A *symposium* is _____.

5. If you write a *synopsis* of a play, you are writing: a parody of the play/a lengthy essay on some aspect of the play/a short summary of the main ideas and events.

ANSWERS

1. arrangement of words in sentences 2. syllogism 3. synthesis 4. meeting to exchange ideas 5. a short summary of the main ideas and events

Now, having mastered this chapter, it might be fun to take another look at the illustration on page 58.

4 Latin Roots

1 ACT, AG, IG: do, drive, carry on, move

Prefixes

de: do the opposite of

Other Roots

lit: law
nav: ship

Suffixes

ary: one who
ate: verb ending
ation: act of
ent: one who
ile: able to
ity: quality of
or: one who

Derivatives

activate (AK tuh vate)
actor (AK ter)
actuary (AK choo air ee)
agent (AY junt)
agile (AJ uhl)
agility (uh JILL uh tee)
agitate (AJ uh tate)
deactivate (dee AK tuh vate)
litigation (lit uh GAY shun)
navigator (NAV uh gay ter)

- **actor**

Because he is "one who moves" about the stage, a person who has a role in a play is called a(n) _____.

- **agent**

After an automobile accident you would call your insurance agent. ("one who does"; one who does things for another person) Another word that literally means "one who does" is *actuary*, which refers to the person who figures rates and risks in an insurance business. Thus, to arrange insurance for your car, you see a(n) _____, whereas the person who calculates how much the company should

- **actuary**

charge for insurance is a(n) _____.

- **the act of carrying on a lawsuit**
  lit: law
  ig: carry on
  ation: act of

To get money back for damages to your car, you may find yourself involved in *litigation*. What is *litigation*? _____

- **agile**

Which derivative means literally "able to move" and is often used to describe cats because they move with such grace and ease? _____ In general, young people have more

- **agility**

_____ than older people. (ability to move easily)

- **agitates**

Washing machines clean clothes by moving them around in soapy water. Another way to say it is that a washing machine _____ the clothes. (drives or moves)

- **nervous or upset**

Agitated can also be applied to people. In the sentence, "After their argument he remained in an agitated state for hours," the word *agitated* means: busy/inactive/nervous or upset.

- **drives or moves a ship**

A *navigator* is literally a person who _____. Actually the navigator *guides* a ship from place to place. This meaning has been extended, so that a person who guides a plane is also called a(n)

- **navigator**

_____.

- **He put the machine into operation**

At the beginning of the dyeing process, the foreman pulled a switch that *activated* the machine. What did he do? _____

- **It is taken out of use**

When a naval ship is no longer to be used, it is *deactivated*. What happens to the ship? _____

SELF-TEST

1. I didn't think that my grandfather would have the _____ to perform rock-and-roll dance movements. (ability to move easily)

2. Health issues have kept cigarette companies involved in *litigation* for decades, with no end in sight. *Litigation* is _____.

3. My insurance agent said if I wished to reapply for coverage after my policy lapsed that a(n) _____ would have to determine new rates. ("one who does")

4. Each ship of that size is assigned two *navigators.* What is a navigator's job? To _____.

5. Fifteen hundred people were put out of work when the war plant was deactivated. *Deactivated* means _____.

1. agility 2. the act of carrying on a lawsuit 3. actuary 4. guide the ship from place to place 5. taken out of use

---

2 **AM, AMAT: love, loving**

Suffixes
abil: able to
ity: quality of
ory: relating to
ous: marked by

Derivatives
amateur (AM uh ter)
amatory (AM uh tore ee)
amiability (aim ee uh BILL uh tee)
amiable (AIM ee uh buhl)
amity (AY muh tee)
amorous (AM uh russ)
amour (uh MORE)

- **love**

- **amateur**

An *amateur* participates in sports or other activities out of _____ for the activity. A beginner is also called a(n) _____.

- **amorous**

People in the mood to make love are said to be _____. (marked by loving)

• **quality of loving; friendliness** *am:* love *abil:* able to *ity:* quality of	His amiability seldom emerges unless he has a few drinks. What is *amiability?* _____
• **amiable**	Those who like other people and get along well with them are _____ people. (relating to loving or liking)
• **warm**	*Amity* between nations means a: warm/cold relationship.
• **amatory**	Casanova was not at all reluctant to discuss his _____ adventures. (relating to love-making)
• **her love affairs**	The publisher told the actress that no one would buy her book unless it told in detail of her *amours.* What do you think the publisher meant? _____

SELF-TEST

1. Susan's sometimes alarming frankness is balanced by her _____. (quality of loving or liking others)

2. "Spare me," he said. "Nothing is as boring to me as hearing about somebody else's _____." (love affairs)

3. Beneath her balcony stood six _____ young men, each ready to serenade her and declare his love. (in the mood to make love)

4. The amity existing between the countries could be destroyed if each continues to violate the territorial rights of the other. *Amity* is _____.

5. Senator Ironton denied having had any *amatory* adventures in Paris. That is, he denied any: spy contacts/wrongdoing/lovemaking.

ANSWERS   1. amiability 2. amours 3. amorous 4. a warm or friendly relationship 5. lovemaking

3   **AQU: water**

Prefixes	**Suffixes**
sub: under	*ous:* characterized by being

Derivatives	aquacade (AK wuh kade)
	aqualung (AK wuh lung)
	aquamarine (AK wuh muh REEN)
	aquaplane (AK wuh plane)
	aquarium (uh QUARE ee um)
	aquatic (uh QUAT ik)
	aqueous (AK wee us)
	subaqueous (sub AK wee us)

• **water**

Aquatic plants must have their roots in _____.

• **under the water**
sub: under
aqu: water

Subaqueous plants are plants that grow where? _____

• **aqualung**

A device that allows divers to breathe below water is a(n) _____. ("water lung")

• **water**

If you are *aquaplaning* you are on a board being towed swiftly across _____.

• **aquarium**

Terra means "land." Thus, a *terrarium* is a thing or place relating to land—an enclosure for keeping animals or plants indoors. What word is used for an enclosure used for fish and other creatures of the sea?

_____

• **blue-green, like seawater**

If "marine" refers to the sea, the color *aquamarine* would be: orange/purplish/blue-green.

• **aqueous**

If a medicine is dissolved in water, it forms a(n) _____ solution. ("having the quality of water") *Aqueous* applies only to chemical solutions.

• **water sports, such as swimming and diving**

A form of entertainment called an *aquacade* originated in Cleveland, Ohio, in 1937. It employed music and featured what kind of sports?

_____

SELF-TEST

1. These new blue-green fabrics are available in peacock blue, forest green, and _____. (bluish-green like seawater)

2. Waterlilies and water hyacinths will be planted in the new
_____ **garden.** (relating to water; needing a water environment)

3. What is the main characteristic of *subaqueous* plants?
_____

4. If chemical or medicine forms an *aqueous* solution, that means it is
_____.

5. Uncle Bert brought me a sea snail and some guppies for my new
_____ **in the living room.** (enclosure for water animals)

ANSWERS

1. aquamarine 2. aquatic 3. they live and grow under the surface of the water 4. dissolved in water 5. aquarium

4 BENE: good

Other Roots

dict: say, speak, tell
fact: do, make
fic: do, make
fit: do, make
ign: do, drive, carry on
vol: will, attitude

Suffixes

ant: one who
ent: marked by
ion: act of
or: one who

Derivatives

benediction (ben uh DIK shun)
benefaction (ben uh FAK shun)
benefactor (BEN uh fak ter)
beneficiary (ben uh FISH ee air ee)
benefit (BEN uh fit)
benevolent (buh NEV uh lunt)
benign (buh NINE)

• **good**
  bene: good
  fit: make

If you *benefit* someone else, you do her some _____.

• **blesses them**

A dying father gives his children a *benediction.* If dict means "speak,"
he: scolds them/blesses them.

- **good**
  bene: good
  vol: will
  ent: marked by

A *benevolent* attitude is one that wishes _____ for others. A free clinic would be a *benevolent* organization.

- **good**

You are your grandfather's favorite. In his will he has designated you as his chief *beneficiary.* You are the one to whom he is going to do some _____. In this case, you will receive part of the estate from your grandfather, who is your benefactor.

- **someone who does good things**

If *factor* means "one who does," what is a *benefactor?*
_____

- **benefaction**

You are grateful for his act of doing good—that is, for his _____.

- **benign**

A *malignant* tumor continues to grow—literally, it does (*ig*) evil (*mal*) marked by (*ant*). What kind of tumor does not continue to grow or cause further trouble? _____ From the meaning "not harmful" the word *benign* has also come to mean "gentle" (a *benign* old woman) or even "favorable" (a *benign* climate).

SELF-TEST

1. Ms. Marshall and her friends consider their club to be a kind of _____ society for helping orphans. (showing good will through actions)

2. Compared with the radical new government that was replacing it, the old empire seemed almost benign. *Benign* means _____.

3. Howard was a proud man, and he actually seemed to resent his father-in-law's frequent benefactions. A *benefaction* is _____.

4. The proceeds from the auction will be used to benefit public television. What does *benefit* mean? _____

5. Mrs. Madison's will was contested because she did not name any of her children as the _____ of her estate. (ones to whom something good is done; persons who receive money or property from a will)

ANSWERS

1. benevolent 2. gentle; favorable; not harmful 3. an act of doing good 4. do good for
5. beneficiaries

5   CAP(T), CEPT, CIP, CEIV, CEIT: seize, take

Prefixes	**Suffixes**
con: with, together	*ate:* verb ending
de: down, away	*ent:* one who
in: not	*ity:* ability to
per: through, thoroughly	*ion:* act of
re: again, back	

Derivatives   capacity (kuh PASS uh tee)
captivate (KAP tuh vate)
capture (KAP chure)
conceit (kun SEAT)
deceive (dee SEEVE)
incapacitate (in kuh PASS uh tate)
perception (per SEP shun)
receipt (ree SEAT)
recipient (ree SIP ee unt)

- take or seize

If you *capture* someone's attention, you _____ it.

- interesting or charming

A *captivating* performance by an actress is: interesting or charming/dull and boring.

- perception
  per: thoroughly
  cept: seize
  ion: act of

The abbreviation ESP stands for extrasensory _____.
(act of thoroughly seizing or taking an idea)

- It makes him unable to take on his usual work.

A man has an illness that *incapacitates* him for a week. What does the illness do with respect to his job? _____

- capacity

The limit of the ability of a tank to hold gas or liquid is called its _____. (ability to take or seize something)

- A person who "takes back" or receives something (for her effort)

Ms. Bellamy is this year's recipient of the Good Neighbor Award. What does *recipient* mean? _____

- **takes away**
  de: away
  ceive: take

A friend deceives you. Literally, he "_____" your faith in him.

- **receipt**

Pay the cashier and take your _____ to the loading dock when you claim your merchandise. ("that which is taken back"; a written statement or ticket acknowledging that money has been paid for goods)

- **conceit**

Laura Lee's personality is flawed by her _____. (state of being taken with herself; high opinion of herself)

SELF-TEST

1. The injury to his back left Randall incapacitated for six weeks. *Incapacitated* means _____.

2. Professor Dundee is a woman of very quick _____. (ability to seize an idea thoroughly)

3. The recipients of the prizes all made brief speeches of appreciation. A *recipient* is _____.

4. I can no longer trust her because she once _____ me. ("took away" trust)

5. Most babies simply do not have the capacity to hold that much food at one time. What does *capacity* mean? _____

6. Did you ever see such _____ in a person! (excessively high opinion of oneself)

ANSWERS

1. unable to take on his usual work 2. perception 3. one who receives or "takes back" 4. deceived 5. ability to take 6. conceit

6 **CAPIT: head**

Prefixes
de: off, down
per: by
re: again, back

Derivatives capital (KAP uh tuhl)
capitol (KAP uh tuhl)
captain (KAP tun)
decapitate (de KAP uh tate)
decapitation (de kap uh TAY shun)
per capita (per KAP uh tuh)
recapitulate (ree kuh PIT choo late)

- **person**
  per: by
  capit: head

The *per capita* consumption of alcohol means the average amount consumed by each _____.

- **captain**

The "head player" of a football team is its _____.
(Here the "i" is dropped from *capit*. You should be able to tell the difference between *capt,* "head," and *capt,* "seize," from the context or setting of a word.)

- **the city**

- **the building that houses the legislature**

The *capital* of a state is its head city, which is the seat of the state government. The actual building housing the legislature is called the *capitol*. If a newspaperman reports a riot in the state *capital*, he means _____; if he reports earthquake damage to the state *capitol*, he means _____.

- **main points or head ideas**

A professor *recapitulates* his lecture of the previous day. He summarizes it briefly by repeating the _____.

- **taking off the head**

In eighteenth-century France a common sentence for criminals was decapitation. What do you think *decapitation* is?

_____

- **decapitated**

Capital punishment is the head or most severe punishment that can be given—that is, death. Complete this gruesome pun: In France the head punishment is to be _____ on the guillotine.
(beheaded)

SELF-TEST

1. The lawyer *recapitulated* the confusing evidence in a manner favorable to his client. What did the lawyer do? _____

2. Recent research has indicated a disturbing increase in the _____ consumption of cigarettes by teenage girls.
(by each person)

3. A group of pickets tried to bar the entrance to the state capitol. What does *capitol* refer to? _____

4. Senator Hopkins and her family moved to the state _____ last August. (head city)

5. The French court sentenced the two criminals to death by *decapitation.* The criminals are to suffer what punishment?

_____

ANSWERS   1. reviewed the main points 2. per capita 3. the actual building housing a legislature
4. capital 5. their heads are to be cut off

7   CARN: flesh

Prefixes	Suffixes
in: in, into	*age:* result of
re: again, back	*al:* relating to
	ation: act of
	ous: relating to

Derivatives   carnage (KAR nij)
carnal (KARN uhl)
carnation (kar NAY shun)
carne (KAR nay)
carnivore (KAR nuh vore)
carnivorous (kar NIV er us)
incarnation (in kar NAY shun)
reincarnation (ree in kar NAY shun)

• **flesh**   The carnation derives its original name from its pale pink or _____ color.

• **flesh**   Carnal desires are desires of the _____.

• **flesh, or meat**   *Chile con carne* is a Mexican dish—literally, chili with _____.

• **flesh-eating**   *Vor* means "eat." What do you think *carnivorous* means?

_____

• **carnivores**   Lions and tigers are flesh-eaters or _____.

• **have been killed or**   A military commander who surveys the *carnage* after a battle looks at a
  slaughtered   great number of people who _____.

• **flesh**   Another way to say that a young man represents an ideal is to say that
                              he is the *incarnation* of the ideal (the ideal put into _____).

• **reincarnation**   Some people believe that each of us is reborn into a succession of dif-
  re: again   ferent bodies. The belief that we are "made into flesh again" is called
  in: into   _____.
  carn: flesh

SELF-TEST   1. Many pet owners are extremely upset when their cats catch birds, for-
                    getting that cats are, after all, _____.

                 2. The Sons of Satan believe that their current leader is the
                    _____ of the devil. (act of being reborn)

                 3. The carnage of World War I brought about a wave of disillusionment
                    and cynicism among young intellectuals both here and in Europe.
                    Carnage refers to _____.

                 4. The sight of her swaying, semi-nude body filled him with
                    _____ desire. (of the flesh)

                 5. We sat around the fireplace eating large bowls of *chile con carne,*
                    which actually means "chili with _____."

ANSWERS   1. flesh-eaters 2. reincarnation 3. slaughter; killing 4. carnal 5. meat, or flesh

8   **CEDE, CEED, CESS: go, move, yield**

Prefixes
ac: to, toward
con: with, together
ex: outside
inter: between
pre: before
pro: forward, in front of, in favor of
re: again, back
se: away from
suc: under
un: not

Derivatives accede (Ak SEED)
cede (SEED)
concede (kuhn SEED)
exceed (ex SEED)
intercede (in ter SEED)
precede (pre SEED)
precedent (PRESS uh dunt)
proceed (pro SEED)
recede (ree SEED)
recession (ree SESS shun)
secede (see SEED)
succeed (suck SEED)
unprecedented (un PRESS uh dent ud)

- **precede**
  pre: before
  cede: go

Mr. Perkins will _____ Ms. Dole on the speaker's platform. **(go before)**

- **receded**
  re: back
  cede: move

After the flood the water quickly _____. (moved back).

- **moved between**
  inter: between
  cede: move

The congresswoman interceded to stop the closing of the Air Force base. *Interceded* means _____.

- **accede**
  ac: toward
  cede: yield

Mary will usually _____ to a reasonable request. (yield toward, meaning to agree voluntarily)

- **conceded**
  con: with
  cede: yield

Seeing that he could not possibly win, Sam _____ the game to Fred. (yield with, meaning to be forced to agree)

- **secede**
  se: away from
  cede: move

The South once tried to _____ from the Union. (move away from a group without the group's approval)

- **went forward**

They proceeded with the work in the usual manner. *Proceeded* means _____.

- **exceed**

Employees are rewarded with a small bonus if they _____ their quota of work for the month. (move outside, go beyond)

- **going back**

When interest rates rise too high, business activity slows, and the economy enters a recession. *Recession* literally means _____.

- **precedent**

When the Supreme Court makes a new decision, it establishes a legal _____ that is followed by all the lower courts. (that which goes before and sets a model or pattern)

- **breaks the old record**

If a team wins an *unprecedented* number of its games, it: establishes the old record/breaks the old record.

SELF-TEST

1. Hester forced the minister to concede that he had been wrong. *Concede* means _____.

2. If Mr. Brooks accedes to the plan, he will provide the money. *Accede* means _____.

3. People are now buying guns in _____ numbers. (breaking the earlier record or pattern)

4. Economists will gather in Washington, D.C., to discuss methods of avoiding another _____. (act of moving backward)

5. The First Lady broke *precedent* by heading a presidential commission. What is a *precedent*? _____

6. The borough of Staten Island took steps to _____ from New York City. (leave a group without that group's approval)

7. It is wise not to _____ in a quarrel between a husband and wife. (move between to bring about an agreement)

8. As the water *receded*, it took the sand with it. That is, the water: rose higher/got lower.

9. The cost of the new missile _____ the Pentagon's original estimate. (goes beyond)

10. After visiting the museum, we will _____ to a quaint little cafe for lunch. (move forward)

ANSWERS

1. to admit or agree under pressure; "yield with" 2. to agree voluntarily; to move toward 3. unprecedented 4. recession 5. custom; that which goes before and sets a model or pattern to be followed 6. secede 7. intercede 8. got lower 9. exceeds 10. proceed

9   CLAM, CLAIM: cry, shout

Prefixes
dis: apart, not
ex: out
pro: forward
re: again, back

Suffixes
ant: one who
ation: act of

Derivatives
claimant (CLAIM unt)
clamor (KLAM er)
clamorous (KLAM er us)
disclaim (dis CLAIM)
exclaim (eks CLAIM)
exclamation (ex kluh MAY shun)
proclaim (pro CLAIM)
proclamation (prok luh MAY shun)
reclaim (ree CLAIM)
reclamation (rek luh MAY shun)

• **crying or shouting**

The *clamor* of people in the street would be what kind of noise?

_____

• **loud and noisy**

A proposal to open a halfway house in the neighborhood is beset by a group of *clamorous* protesters. They are: disorganized and unruly/loud and noisy.

• **reclaim**
re: back
claim: cry

To claim something, you visualize yourself saying, "Hey, that's mine!" Nowadays the claiming more often takes the form of a ticket or paper with your name or identifying number written on it. When you surrender your luggage at an airline ticket counter, you are given a claim ticket in return. At the end of your trip you _____ your luggage. (claim again; "shout back")

• **put it back into pro-
ductive use**

Environmentalists have undertaken the *reclamation* of land after years of toxic dumping. What are they attempting to do with the land?

_____

• **claimant**

A claim check identifies you as the _____. (one who makes a claim to something)

- **disclaims**
  dis: apart
  claim: cry

If you read the fine print on the claim ticket, you will learn that the issuing company _____ responsibility ("cries itself apart from"; denies) beyond the limits set forth in the claim ticket.

- **shouted forth**
  pro: forward

After he was accused of taking bribes, the mayor *proclaimed* his innocence. *Proclaimed* literally means _____.

- **Proclamation**

The slaves were freed by the Emancipation _____.
(act of shouting forward; public announcement)

- **exclaim**

Suddenly you run into an old friend you have not seen for years. You _____ (shout out), "How wonderful to see you again!" Your _____ (act of crying or shouting out) is probably matched by one from your friend.

- **exclamation**

SELF-TEST

1. Tim's concentration was continually interrupted by the _____ of people enjoying a cocktail party in the patio next door. (noise made by shouting or loud talking)

2. When any of his constituents had performed some great act of service to the community, Senator Markowitz honored the person with a *proclamation* from the state senate. What is a *proclamation*? _____

3. She brought with her an original copy of the insurance policy to establish that she was indeed the _____. (one who claims)

4. Norman said he did not know about the mistake and *disclaimed* any responsibility for it. That is, he: denied/accepted/laughed at any responsibility.

5. What is the purpose of slum *reclamation*? _____

6. The strongest _____ she ever uttered was "Oh fudge." (act of shouting out; sharp or sudden utterance)

ANSWERS

1. clamor 2. a public announcement; "a shouting forth" 3. claimant 4. denied; "cried apart" 5. to put a neighborhood or district back into productive use 6. exclamation

10   CORP: body

Prefixes
in: in or not

Suffixes
al: relating to
ate: verb ending
cle: noun ending (little thing)
ent: marked by
us: noun ending

Derivatives
corporal (KORE per uhl)
corporation (KORE pore AY shun)
corporeal (kore PORE ee uhl)
corps (KORE)
corpse (KORPSS)
corpulent (KORE pew luhnt)
corpus (KORE puhss)
corpuscle (KORE puss uhl)
incorporate (in KORE per ate)
incorporeal (in kore PORE ee uhl)

- **body**
  corp: body

- **corps**

- **body**
  corp: body
  us: noun ending
  cle: little thing

- **body**

- **incorporeal**

- **body**

The Marine *Corps* is a military _____. It usually consists of two or more divisions. The plural form is the same as the singular: The parade will be attended by members of all the military _____.

A *corpuscle* is a "little _____" or cell that floats in the blood or lymph. It carries oxygen and carbon dioxide, and it helps destroy disease germs.

Corporal punishment is inflicted on the: body/mind.

Corporeal things are "bodily" or material. They can be seen and touched. Things such as ghosts or spirits that can neither be seen nor touched are _____. (not corporeal)

In law the body of a murdered person is called the *corpus delicti*— "the _____ of the crime"—and is the fact that proves a crime has been committed.

• corpulent   Overweight people would probably prefer to think of themselves as being _____. It is a more clinical-sounding term and therefore less offensive to them.

• corpus   A complete collection of writings, laws, and the like is called a(n) _____. (Latin for *body*)

• made into or put into one body   Frank's various experiences with Alaskan wolves have been incorporated into a novel. What does *incorporate* mean here?

_____

SELF-TEST

1. At last! Fashion styles for corpulent men. *Corpulent* means: skinny/middle-aged/fat.

2. Your suggestion will be _____ into this new plan. (made part of; put into one body)

3. The spiritual medium promised that the room would be full of _____ beings with whom only she could communicate. (not having a physical body)

4. To say the least, Aunt Polly was generous with corporal punishment. What is *corporal* punishment? _____

5. The marching bands were supplied by the Army and Navy and Marine _____. (bodies)

6. Perry Mason asked the judge to dismiss the case unless the prosecuting attorney produced the corpus delicti. Here *corpus* refers to _____.

7. That short story should certainly be featured in the Hemingway _____. (body; collection of writings)

8. The blood test revealed that I am low in white corpuscles. What are *corpuscles*? _____

ANSWERS   1. fat 2. incorporated 3. incorporeal 4. punishment inflicted on the body 5. Corps 6. the body (of the murdered person) 7. corpus 8. "little bodies"; cells that help fight disease germs

11   CLUD, CLUS, CLOIS, CLAUS: shut, close

Prefixes	**Other Roots**	**Suffixes**
ex: out	*mal:* bad	*ion:* act of
in: in	*phobia:* fear	
oc: against		
pre: before		
re: again, back		
se: away		

Derivatives   claustrophobia (klaus truh FOBE ee uh)
cloister (KLOY ster)
exclude (eks KLUDE)
include (in KLUDE)
malocclusion (mal uh KLUZE shun)
preclude (pre KLUDE)
recluse (REK loose)
seclude (see KLUDE)

- **include**
  in: in
  clud: shut

Our plans also _____ you. (shut in; enclose)

- **excluded**
  ex: out
  clud: shut

Thirty years ago, women were _____ from the club.
(shut out)

- **shut away; isolated**

They built their cabin in a *secluded* spot. What kind of spot was it?

_____

- **precluded**

A lack of money _____ the possibility of their tak-
ing a pleasure cruise this year. (shut before; prevented ahead of time)

- **someone "shut back"
  from public view**

Emily Dickinson, famous American poet, preferred to live as a recluse.
What is a *recluse?* _____

- **claustrophobia**

Sailors who suffer from _____ are unsuited to submarine duty. (a phobia about closed places)

- a place shut off from the world

The disillusioned princess spent the rest of her life in a religious *cloister*. What kind of place do you think a *cloister* is? _____

- malocclusion

Hilda's teeth do not shut against each other properly. Her problem is known as _____. ("bad closing")

SELF-TEST

1. Having been born outside the United States _____ my children from ever becoming president. (prevented ahead of time)

2. For nearly six years Hawthorne seldom left his room, and many of his relatives and friends thought he had become a(n) _____ for life. (person who shuts himself back from the world)

3. She dislikes riding in elevators because she is subject to *claustro-phobia*, which is _____.

4. What kind of dental problem is *malocclusion?* _____

5. The young lovers often met in a(n) _____ part of the park. (isolated)

6. Both a monastery and a convent are examples of a(n) _____. (place shut off from the world)

ANSWERS

1. precludes 2. recluse 3. fear of being shut in 4. The teeth do not shut against each other properly; there is a poor "bite." 5. secluded 6. cloister

12   CRED: believe

Prefixes
in: not

Suffixes
able: able to
ible: able to
ity: state of
ous: marked by

Derivatives
credence (KREED unce)
credible (KRED uh buhl)

creditable (KRED uh tuh buhl)
credulous (KREJ uh luss)
creed (KREED)
incredible (in KRED uh buhl)
incredulity (in kruh DUEL uh tee)
incredulous (in KREJ uh luss)

- **believes**

Whether it is religious, political, or personal, a *creed* is a statement of the principles or fundamentals someone _____.

- **credible**
  cred: believe
  ible: able

John gives us a long story to explain his lateness. If his story is believable, we say it is _____.

- **incredible**
  in: not

If it is unbelievable, we say it is _____.

A *credulous* person is one who believes things too readily. ("It must be true. I read it in the paper!") When something amazing happens, when you can hardly believe what you see or hear, an *incredulous* expression comes over your face. If a little green man with horns suddenly materialized before you, no doubt you would be overcome with a feeling of *incredulity*.

- **believable**
- **not believable**
- **credulous**
  cred: believe
  ous: marked by

To summarize: Something that is credible is _____. Something incredible is _____. A person who believes too easily is _____.

- **incredulous**

- **incredulity**

Something that you cannot at first believe, in spite of evidence, brings about a(n) _____ look to your face; it creates in you a feeling of _____.

- **believability**

The testimony of two other reliable witnesses lent credence to my story about sighting a flying saucer. What does *credence* mean here?

_____

- **creditable**

The actor gave a very _____ performance as Hamlet. (able to be believed; deserving credit or praise)

SELF-TEST

1. Bill's account of the adventure was so _____ that none of us could take him seriously. (not believable)

2. Ten minutes after she received the check for one million dollars she still had an incredulous expression on her face. *Incredulous* means _____.

3. The pediatrician gave little *credence* to the boy's story that he had swallowed the quarter. The doctor thought the story was: likely/unlikely/confirmed.

4. Vera did a very _____ job of writing up that report for the manager. (praiseworthy)

5. Teddy admitted readily that his actions were not in keeping with the Boy Scout creed. A *creed* is _____.

ANSWERS

1. incredible 2. not believing 3. unlikely 4. creditable 5. a statement of belief

13   CUR, COUR: run

Prefixes

con: with, together
ex: outside
in: in, into
pre: before
re: again, back

Suffixes

ier: one who
ent: marked by; that which
ion: act of
ly: adverb ending
or: that which
ory: marked by

Derivatives

concurrently (kuhn KUR runt lee)
courier (KUR ee er)
current (KUR runt)
cursive (KUR sive)
cursor (KUR ser)
cursory (KURSS er ree)
excursion (eks KUR shun)
incursion (in KUR shun)
precursor (pre KUR sir)
recurrent (re KUR runt)

• **current**

cur: run
ent: that which

It is more difficult to swim against the _____. ("that which runs"; running part of a stream; the swiftest part)

- **marked by running back**

Marvin suffered from a recurrent illness. *Recurrent* literally means _____. So a recurrent illness occurs again and again.

- **excursion**

They planned a brief _____ into the countryside. (act of running outside)

- **acts of running into; invasions**

The newspaper reported the latest incursions of enemy forces. What are *incursions?* _____

- **cursory**

Selma could not answer the question directed to her because she had given the article only a(n) _____ glance. (running)

- **that which runs before**

A small power blackout in the East may be the precursor of widespread power failures. A *precursor* is what? _____

- **courier**

A(n) _____ arrived with a message from the king. (one who runs; runner)

- **concurrently**
  con: together
- *less*

A felon serving several sentences _____ will spend more/less time in jail than someone serving them consecutively.

SELF-TEST

1. Since his automobile crash, Mr. Small has been plagued by _____ nightmares. (occurring again and again)

2. The ambassador laughed and admitted she was acting as little more than a diplomatic courier, bringing an important message from the president for the new premier. What is a *courier?* _____

3. The local shopkeepers thought that the new mall was an enemy _____ into their territory. (act of running into; invasion)

4. The slowdown in housing sales may be the *precursor* of a recession. *Precursor* means _____.

5. The convention headquarters in the new Hilton hotel are large enough that three large groups can be accommodated concurrently. What does *concurrently* mean? _____

6. Amanda's Tours specializes in one-day _____ for senior citizens. (acts of running outside)

ANSWERS   1. recurrent 2. a runner or messenger 3. incursion 4. that which runs before 5. running together 6. excursions

14 DICT: say, speak, tell

Prefixes	Other Roots	Suffixes
e: out	*phone:* instrument for recording sound	*ate:* verb ending
pre: before	*juris:* law	*ian:* one who
	val: farewell	*or:* one who

Derivatives

dictaphone (DIK tuh fone)
dictate (DIK tate)
dictator (DIK tate er)
edict (EE dikt)
jurisdiction (jure iss DIK shun)
predicate (PRED uh kate)
valedictorian (val uh dik TORE ee un)

• **he speaks it to her**   When a boss *dictates* a letter to his stenographer, what does he do?
_____

• **one who speaks**   The *dictator* of a country is literally _____. In
dict: speak   actual usage, a *dictator* is a very powerful person who *tells* everyone
or: one who   else what to do.

• **valedictorian**   *Vale* means "farewell." The person who delivers the farewell address
for a graduating class is the _____. (Traditionally,
he or she is also the student with the highest grade average.)

• **based on**   The prince's early education was predicated on a study of Latin and
Greek. Here *predicated* means that someone in authority (his parents or
his tutors) spoke about the matter ahead of time and made a decision
which was then followed. Thus, *predicated* means: based on/arranged.

• **jurisdiction**   *Juris* means "law." If something is outside the area in which a court
can hear and decide ("speak on") cases, it is outside that court's
_____.

• **speaks out**   An *edict* is something that _____ on a subject.
e: out   Actually an edict is a command or order.

SELF-TEST   1. The judge said that such a matter was entirely outside the jurisdiction
of her court. *Jurisdiction* refers to _____.

2. The Cold War was *predicated* on the conflict between Communism and democracy. *Predicated* means _____.

3. The controversy was finally resolved by royal _____. (act of speaking out; decision made by one in authority)

4. The opposition party feared that the new president was intent on becoming a(n) _____. (one ruling absolutely)

5. Nancie Jane is this year's valedictorian. What does the *valedictorian* normally do at graduation? _____

6. Before she went out, Mrs. Jones _____ a list of instructions to the baby-sitter. (spoke, said).

1. the area in which a court can hear and decide on a case 2. based on; "spoken before" 3. edict 4. dictator 5. gives a farewell address 6. dictated

15   DUCT, DUC: lead

Prefixes
con: with, together
de: down, away
in: in
re: again, back
se: away

Other Roots
aqu: water
via: road

Suffixes
ile: marked by
ive: marked by
ion: act of, process

Derivatives
aqueduct (AK wuh dukt)
conduct (kun DUKT)
deduce (dee DUCE)
duct (DUKT)
ductile (DUK tuhl)
induction (in DUK shun)
reduce (re DUCE)
seduce (sih DUCE)
seductive (sih DUK tiv)
viaduct (VEYE uh dukt)

• **conduct**
con: together
duct: lead

John Masters will _____ the orchestra. (lead together)

• **led back**
re: back
duc: lead

The cost of personal computers has been reduced considerably. *Reduced* literally means _____.

• **seduced**

In the narrowest sense *seduce* means "lead astray" sexually: John *seduced* Mary. In a broader sense it means simply to lead into wrong-doing. The adjective form *seductive,* on the other hand, describes something that allures or charms: *seductive* music, a *seductive* manner of speaking. To review, a friend _____ you into disregarding your work and going to a movie. The movie was filled with

• **seductive**

_____ brown-eyed maidens swaying to the rhythm of tropical drums.

• **bent**
  duct: lead

Ductile metals like copper can be easily: bent/hardened. This is because their pliability allows for stretching and reshaping.

• **ducts**

The channels that allow tears to flow from the eyes are called tear _____. ("leaders")

• **leads water**
  aque: water
  duct: lead

The Romans gave us the *aqueduct,* which is a structure that _____.

• **viaduct**

A structure used to lead a road *(via)* or train track across a valley, a gorge, or a part of a city is a(n) _____.

• **induction**

The name given to the process whereby civilians are "led into" the armed services is called _____.

• **deduced**

If you *deduce* that someone is a Republican, your logic leads down from a generalization (Everyone here at the meeting is a Republican) to a specific case (John must be a Republican). Sherlock Holmes knew that a man who limps puts more weight on his good leg. In investigating a murder, Sherlock found footprints in the mud outside a library window. The impression of the left foot was much deeper. Sherlock therefore _____ that the murderer was lame in the right leg. ("led down")

SELF-TEST

1. The _____ fragrance of her perfume overcame his resolve to study for the exam. (alluring; tending to lead astray)

2. Sherlock Holmes _____ that the thief must have been lefthanded. ("led down"; inferred from a general principle)

3. Two days after he reached the age of 21 the army ordered him to report for induction. What is *induction*? _____

4. Copper is a ductile metal. What does *ductile* mean?

_____

5. What is the function of an air *duct*? _____

6. What would you call a structure that leads a road over a deep gorge?

_____

7. Before the invention of the _____ the land was too arid to be farmed. (structures that carry water)

8. The warm, sunny weather seduced me into leaving the library and going outdoors. *Seduced* means _____

ANSWERS

1. seductive 2. deduced 3. the process of being led into the armed forces 4. easily bent 5. to lead or bring air into a room 6. viaduct 7. aqueduct 8. led astray; persuaded into some form of wrongdoing

16 FAC, FACT, FECT, FIC, FEAT, FEAS, FY: do, make

Prefixes	Other Roots	Suffixes
ef: out	*magn:* large	*ile:* able
per: through, thoroughly	*manu:* hand	*ity:* quality of
pro: forward, in front of, in favor of		*ient:* marked by
		ion: act of
		ist: one who
		ory: place

Derivatives
efficient (ee FISH unt)
facile (FASS uhl)
facility (fuh SILL uh tee)
facsimile (fak SIM uh lee)
factory (FAK tree)
feasible (FEEZ uh buhl)
feat (FEET)
magnify (MAG nuh feye)
manufacture (man yoo FAK chure)
perfectionist (per FEK shun ist)
proficient (pro FISH unt)

• **factory**
fact: made
ory: place

A place where things are made is a(n) _____.

- **to make by hand**
  manu: hand
  fact: made

If *manu* means "hand," what is the literal meaning of the verb *manufacture?* _____

- **ease**

- **facility**

A *facile* artist is "able to do"—that is, able to create things with: ease/difficulty. An ease at doing or making something is called a(n) _____.

- **a copy or reproduction**
  fac: make
  simil: similar

An American millionaire builds a home in New York that is a facsimile of a castle in Europe. If *simil* means "similar," what is a *facsimile?* _____. The *fax* machine, indispensible in modern business, is named for an abbreviation of facsimile.

- **perfectionist**
  per: thoroughly
  fect: do
  ion: act of
  ist: one who

A person who has to do everything as thoroughly as possible is called a(n) _____. (one who does thoroughly)

- **proficient**
  pro: forward
  fic: do

If you can do something that requires skill or knowledge, you are _____. (marked by making forward—that is, by making progress)

- **efficient**
  ef: out

If you can do something without wasting time, money, or energy, you are _____. ("marked by making out"; able to bring about desired effects).

- **make larger**
  magn: large
  fy: make

To *magnify* is to _____.

- **classify**

To group things into classes is to _____. ("make classes")

- **done or made**
  feas: do, make

If something is *feasible,* it can be _____.

- **feats**

Audiences generally applaud "things done" that show great strength or skill, such as acrobatic _____.

SELF-TEST

1. Henry and his brother William were both *facile* writers. That is, they both wrote: poetically/strangely/easily.

2. The rare book dealer said our copy was merely a *facsimile* of the first edition. What is a *facsimile?* _____

3. Stokes has a(n) _____ for inspiring others to make a greater effort. (ease of doing something)

4. A(n) _____ secretary would organize the office routine in such a way that everything got done on time with a minimum of effort. (able to bring about an effect without wasting time or energy)

5. Margaret told Harry that the TV comedy series "The Odd Couple" is a story about a slob and a perfectionist who try to live together. A *perfectionist* is someone who _____.

6. Only a very _____ craftsman like Mr. Donovan could command such a high fee for his work. (able to make progress; having skill or knowledge)

7. Ms. Martin questioned whether or not it would be feasible to tear out the west wall of the delivery room. *Feasible* means _____.

8. Righting that overturned car was certainly a(n) _____ of strength! ("thing done")

ANSWERS 1. easily 2. a copy or reproduction 3. facility 4. efficient 5. feels he must do everything as thoroughly as possible 6. proficient 7. able to be done 8. feat

17 FER, LAT: bear, carry*

Prefixes	Other Roots	Suffixes
de: down, away	*proli:* offspring	*ate:* verb ending
dif: apart, not		*ation:* process of
in: in		*ion:* act of
pro: forward, in front of, in favor of		*ence:* quality of
		ile: marked by
		ial: marked by
		ous: marked by

Derivatives   conifer (KON uh fer)
coniferous (kuh NIF er us)
defer (dee FER)

---

*FER and LAT are grouped together here because they have the same meaning.

deference (DEF er unce)
deferential (def er EN shuhl)
differentiate (dif fer EN she ate)
elation (ee LAY shun)
fertile (FERT uhl)
infer (in FER)
inference (IN fer unce)
proliferate (pro LIF er ate)
proliferation (pro liff er AY shun)
relate (ree LATE)

* **bear**
  fer: bear
  ile: marked by

If an animal is *fertile*, it is able to _____ offspring. To "bear" them, it must "carry" them in embryo form; hence, the similarity of the two meanings.

* **conifer**
  con: cone
  fer: bear

A pine tree, which "bears cones," is a(n) _____.

* **coniferous**

The Norway pine is a(n) _____ tree. (marked by bearing cones)

* **proliferation**

If *proli* means "offspring," the process of reproducing new parts, off-shoots or cells is called _____.

* **more countries are getting them, raising the threat of war or terrorism**

If the president is worried that nuclear weapons are proliferating, why should you worry? _____

* **carry down**
  de: down
  fer: carry

Two of you must make a decision. You decide to defer to your friend. Literally, *defer* means _____. Temporarily you "carry down" your importance to a lower level than his. The voluntary respect you show older people, bosses, and the like is called

* **deference**
* **deferential**

_____. Most of us like it when others treat us in a(n) _____ manner. (marked by deference)

* **carried apart**
  dif: apart
  fer: carry

Two things that are *different* are literally _____. To make a distinction between two things—that is, to carry them apart—is to _____ them.

* **differentiate**

Two women needed to pass through the same door. The first deferred to the second, saying "Age before beauty." She is *implying* that she is the younger and prettier of the two. The second was writer Dorothy Parker, who said, "Pearls before swine."

Parker *implied* that she was a treasure and the other woman was a pig. The one who sends the message with her words *implies* the message. The one who perceives that message *infers* it.

The message that is *implied* is called an *implication*.

The message that is *inferred* is called an *inference*.

• **relate** We listen politely to the psychic _____ his out-of-body experiences until we couldn't contain ourselves any longer. (carry back; give an account of)

• **elation** When Sam received his grades for the year and school was over, he felt a sense of _____. ("act of being carried outside" one-self; state of joy or pride)

SELF-TEST

1. The young intern approached the famous surgeon in a(n) _____ manner. (showing respect)

2. If my inference is correct, you imply that I am lazy and irresponsible. What is an *inference*? _____

3. In despair she said, "The problems facing this company keep *proliferating!*" She means that: new problems keep popping up/the problems are getting more difficult/the problems cost more to solve

4. If you have a conscience, you cannot help _____ing between good and bad in your own behavior. (making a distinction)

5. Mr. Dunn planted only conifers because they take less watering. What are *conifers*? _____

6. The rich soil of the delta is said to be very _____. (able to bear offspring)

7. When he was named as the presidential candidate's running mate, the senator expressed his _____ by jumping up and down like the winner of a TV game show.

ANSWERS 1. deferential 2. a process of uncovering a hidden message 3. new problems keep popping up 4. differentiating 5. cone-bearing trees 6. fertile 7. elation

18   FID: faith

Prefixes	Suffixes
af: to, toward	*ant:* one who
con: with, together	*el:* one who
dif: apart, not	*ent:* marked by
e: out	*ion:* act of
in: not	*ity:* act of
per: through, thoroughly	*ous:* marked by

Derivatives   affidavit (af fuh DAY vit)
bona fide (BON uh FIDE)
confidant (kon fuh DAHNT)
confide (kun FIDE)
diffident (DIF uh dunt)
fidelity (fuh DELL uh tee)
infidel (IN fuh dell)
infidelity (in fuh DELL uh tee)
perfidious (per FID ee us)

- **faith**
- **confidant**
  con: with
  fid: faith

When you *confide* in someone, you show that you have complete
_____ in her. The person in whom you most often
confide is your _____. (one you have faith with)

- **faith**

Bona means "good." A *bona fide* offer to buy a house is made "in
good _____."

- **faithfulness (especially sexual)**

The marriage vows require a couple to pledge their *fidelity* to each
other. What does fidelity mean? _____

- **infidelity**

If one of them later breaks that pledge, that person is guilty of
_____.

- **affidavit**
  af: toward
  fid: faith
- **diffident**

A statement written down and sworn to be true is a(n)
_____. ("that which is faithful toward")

A person who is "apart from faith" in himself is very shy or
_____.

- **infidel**

During the Crusades the Christians fought the
_____. (those not of the faith, here the Christian faith)

- **faith**
- **perfidious**

A *perfidious* action breaks _____ with someone:
The legal maneuvers of Ted's partner were _____
because they brought about Ted's financial ruin. (marked by thoroughly breaking faith)

SELF-TEST

1. Ms. Parks insisted that she had received a bona fide invitation to join the law firm of Miller, Sarks, and Warnes. *Bona fide* means _____.

2. In spite of their personality differences, General Patton and General Bradley treated each other as _____. (a person regularly confided in)

3. Ms. Thornton could not appear at the trial, but she left an affidavit. What is an *affidavit*? _____

4. Jack had a reputation for being unfriendly whereas in reality he was simply diffident. *Diffident* means _____.

5. Mr. Horn's action in revealing our plans to the opposition party is _____. (marked by a complete lack of faith)

6. We always offered so many excuses for not attending Sunday school that Aunt Polly branded us her little _____. (those who are not of the faith)

ANSWERS

1. in good faith 2. confidants 3. a written statement sworn to be a faithful account 4. shy; lacking faith 5. perfidious 6. infidels

19 FUS, FUND, FOUND: pour

Prefixes
con: with, together
ef: out
in: in
pro: forward, in front of, in favor of
re: again, back
suf: under

Suffixes
ive: marked by
ry: place where
ion: condition of

Derivatives
confuse (kun FUSE)
effusive (ih FEW siv)
foundry (FOUN dree)

infuse (in FUSE)
profusion (pro FEW zhun)
refund (REE fund)
refuse (re FUSE)
suffuse (suh FUSE)

- **pour back**
  re: back
  fus: pour

He offered his help, but she refused it. *Refuse* is such a common word it is difficult to think of a synonym for it. But its original, literal meaning is vivid: *refuse* means "_____."

- **pour together**
  con: together
  fus: pour

Confuse also has a vivid literal meaning: *confuse* means "_____." Think of that meaning as you read this sentence: He knew that he was aging because his memories often became *confused*.

- **poured into; that is, he inspired his fellow workers**

She infused her own enthusiasm into her fellow workers. What does *infused* mean here? "_____"

- **profusion**

The garden was a(n) _____ of flowers in all colors. (act of pouring forth)

- **suffused**

Just at sunset the clouds were _____ with pink. (poured under; underspread)

- **refund**

In two days you will receive a(n) _____ from the national office. (that which is poured back; money given back)

- **a place where iron is melted and poured into casts**

The workers are going on strike at the iron foundry. What do you think an iron *foundry* is? _____

- **showing much feeling; gushy**
  ef: out
  fus: pour
  ive: marked by

Three days after our disagreement, her greeting was as effusive as ever. Think of the literal meaning of *effusive* and then describe the kind of greeting she gave. _____

SELF-TEST

1. The meadow was covered with a(n) _____ of wild-flowers. (act of pouring forth)

2. The sergeant tried to infuse his men with his own sense of responsibility. *Infuse* means to _____.

3. Their appreciation was so effusive it almost embarrassed him. What does *effusive* mean? _____

4. The flowers were pale cream lightly _____ with pink. (underspread)

5. The statues were sent back to the _____, where they would be melted down and recast. (place where metals are melted and poured into casts)

1. profusion 2. "pour into"; inspire 3. showing more feeling than is warranted; gushing; "pouring out" 4. suffused 5. foundry

20 GRAD, GRESS: step, go

Prefixes

ag: to, toward
de: down, away
di: apart, not
e: out
pro: forward, in front of, in favor of
retro: backward

Suffixes

ive: marked by
ion: act of

Derivatives

aggressive (uh GRESS iv)
degrade (dee GRADE)
digress (deye GRESS)
egress (EE gress)
progressive (pro GRESS iv)
retrogression (RET row gress shun)

• **degrade**
 de: down
 grad: step

If a person's actions make him "step down" to a lower level of behavior or existence, they _____ him.

• **progressive**
 pro: forward
 gress: go

An illness that keeps "going forward" and becoming worse is a(n) _____ illness. *Progressive* can also have a positive meaning, as when a mayor is complimented by being called progressive (going forward; wanting improvement in government)

• **setback or deterio-
  ration**
  retro: backward
  gress: go

An ill person who suffers a general *retrogression* is undergoing a: slow improvement/setback or deterioration.

• **aggressive**
  ag: toward
  gress: step

A person who is quick to assert himself, to "step toward" others, is a(n) _____ person.

• **to turn aside from
  the main subject**
  di: apart
  gress: go

A lecturer is discussing the reasons why the South seceded from the Union. Then she *digresses* and for a few minutes discusses the problems of commuting to and from a large urban center. What does *digress* mean? _____

• **exits**
  e: out
  gress: go

If *egress* from a building is insufficient to satisfy the fire inspector, there are not enough: exits/porters.

SELF-TEST

1. The marble statues and columns in Venice are subject to _____ deterioration and decay. ("marked by going forward"; advancing)

2. The *egress* of cars from the stadium parking lot took almost as long as the game itself. What does *egress* mean? _____

3. The *retrogression* of a man's faculties would mean their: worsening/gradual improvement.

4. The U.S. Trade Representative became more _____ in his negotiations with the Japanese. (determined pursuit of one's own ends; self-assertive)

5. The brainwashing techniques were intended to break down a prisoner's resistance, to _____ him in his own eyes. (to lower in moral or intellectual character; "step down")

6. When her colleague seemed on the verge of digressing, Mildred would cough politely. *Digressing* means _____.

ANSWERS

1. progressive 2. movement to the outside; going out 3. worsening 4. aggressive
5. degrade 6. leaving the main subject in a discussion; "going apart"

21 JAC, JECT: throw, hurl

Prefixes
ab: down
ad: to, toward
con: with, together
de: down, away
e: out
in: in, into
inter: between
ob: against
pro: forward, in front
  of, in favor of
re: back
sub: under, below

Suffixes
ive: that which
ion: act of
ile: that which

Derivatives
abject (AB jekt)
adjective (AJ ik tiv)
conjecture (kun JEK shure)
dejected (dee JEK tuhd)
ejaculation (ee JAK yoo LAY shun)
eject (ee JEKT)
injection (in JEK shun)
interject (in ter JEKT)
objective (ub JEK tive)
project (pro JEKT)
projectile (pro JEK tuhl)
reject (ree JEKT)
subjection (sub JEK shun)

- **ejaculation**
  e: out
  jac: throw

A sudden, brief, often very emotional "throwing out" of words is a(n) _____. A discharge of semen is also called an *ejacu-lation.*

- **hurl forward**
  pro: forward
  ject: throw

If you had a time machine, you could project yourself into the future. Literally, to *project* means to _____.

• **projectile**	An explosive "hurled forward" from a gun, cannon, or bazooka is a(n) _____.
• **act of throwing into**	A nurse administered the injection. *Injection* means _____. In this case, medicine is injected into a patient's body, but a large grant of money to a bankrupt company
• **injection**	might also be called a(n) _____.
• **objective** *ob:* against	What is your educational _____? (thing thrown against; thing aimed at)
• **thrown back; refused** *re:* back	Even though she was down to her last dime, she rejected the offer of a small loan. *Rejected* means _____.
• **adjective**	A(n) _____ modifies a noun, as in "a *tall* tree." (that which is thrown toward)
• **subjection**	The _____ of the mountain tribes took five years. (act of throwing under; bringing under the control of someone else)
• **a guess; literally, "that which is thrown together"**	It is a matter of conjecture whether or not the congressman will run again. What do you think *conjecture* means? _____
• **ejects**	At the mere touch of a button the machine _____ stamps. (throws out)
• **dejected**	*Dejected* and *abject* both have the literal meaning "thrown down," but whereas *dejected* means "lowered in spirits," *abject* means "miserable or wretched." After they lost the game, the team members were _____. The worst kind of poverty is called
• **abject**	_____ poverty.
• **interject**	Wilson tapped Mrs. Bowes on the shoulder and said, "May I please _____ a word or two?" ("throw between")

SELF-TEST

1. Lawrence had packed some snow tightly into a small ball, and he aimed the _____ directly at Mr. Crowe's hat. (object hurled forward)

2. The first rejection slip made him feel _____. (low in spirits)

3. The refugees reported they lived under _____ conditions. (miserable or wretched)

4. Diana dismissed his explanation of the delay in taking off from the airport as mere conjecture. What is a *conjecture?* _____

5. Many cultures accept that women will live in _____ to their men. (condition of being under the influence or control of someone else)

6. Each new job recruit had first to determine her career objective. What is an *objective?* _____

1. projectile 2. dejected 3. abject 4. a guess; something "thrown together" 5. subjection
6. goal aimed at; something to be "thrown against"

22 MAL: bad

Other Roots

dict: say, speak, tell
factor: one who does
feas, fact: do, make
ig: do, drive, carry on
vol: will, attitude

Suffixes

ance: act of
ant: marked by
ion: act of
ous: marked by
or: one who

Derivatives
maladroit (MAL uh droit)
malady (MAL uh dee)
malaria (muh LARE ee uh)
malediction (mal uh DIK shun)
malevolent (muh LEV uh lunt)
malfeasance (mal FEEZ unce)
malefactor (MAL uh fak ter)
malignant (muh LIG nunt)
malnutrition (mal new TRISH un)
malodorous (mal ODE er us)

- **malignant**
  mal: bad
  ig: do

  A tumor that is no longer growing or spreading is benign (of good origin); a harmful, often cancerous tumor is _____.
  (marked by doing bad)

- **curses; "bad speech"**
  mal: bad
  dict: speak

  Because I had not crossed her palm with enough silver, the fortune teller hurled maledictions at me as I left the tent. What are *maledictions?* _____

- **marked by bad will; having an evil intention**
  mal: bad
  vol: will

With a malevolent look in his eye, the bully grabbed Tom's arm. *Malevolent* means _____

- **some kind of wrongdoing**
  feas: do

What is meant by *malfeasance* in public office? _____

- **maladroit**

Adroit people are very graceful, especially in using their bodies. What would people be called who are very clumsy? _____

- **malodorous**

As a protective mechanism skunks throw off a(n) _____ scent. (marked by a bad odor)

- **malnutrition**

An improper diet can lead to _____. (bad nutrition)

- **bad**

Malaria was once thought to be caused by _____ air.

- **one who does something bad**
  mal: bad
  factor: one who does

Teddy Roosevelt blamed many of the country's problems on "malefactors of great wealth." What is a *malefactor*? _____

- **bad**

No one could decide what was the cause of the *malady* that overtook the princess. A *malady* is literally "something _____" —an illness or a disease.

SELF-TEST

1. In two days the dead fish were _____, to say the least. (bad-smelling)

2. Shakespeare portrays Shylock as a malevolent old man who wants revenge in the form of a pound of human flesh. *Malevolent* means _____.

3. For years he has been suffering from a mysterious _____. (sickness, disease)

4. The mismanagement of the county treasury was attributed to incompetence, not *malfeasance*. Malfeasance is _____.

5. Ms. Taylor is too maladroit to be a good waitress. *Maladroit* means: clumsy/money-hungry/young.

6. As she hurried down the stairs, she could hear the old drunk's _____ ringing in her ears. (curses)

7. Eventually the old colonel became so twisted in mind that he thought anyone who opposed him in any way whatsoever was a malefactor. What is a *malefactor?* _____

1. malodorous 2. marked by bad will or evil intentions 3. malady 4. wrongdoing 5. clumsy 6. maledictions 7. someone who does evil things

23 MIT, MISS: send

Prefixes

ad: to, toward
com: with, together
e: out
inter: between
pre: before
pro: forward, in front of, in favor of
re: again, back
sub: under
trans: across, through, beyond

Suffixes

ance: that which
ary: one who
ile: that which
ion: act of
ive: that which

Derivatives

admit (ad MIT)
commission (kum MISH un)
emissary (EM uh sare ee)
emission (ee MISH un)
intermission (in ter MISH un)
missile (MISS uhl)
missive (MISS iv)
premise (PREM iss)
promise (PROM iss)
remission (ree MISH un)
remittance (ree MIT unce)
submissive (sub MISS iv)
transmit (trans MIT)

Choose the derivatives that fit the literal meanings listed below:

(Money) sent back: _____

• **remittance**
re: back
mit: send

- **transmit**   To send across, as a message: _____

- **promise**   A guarantee "sent forth": _____

- **intermission**   A period of time "sent between," as at a play or concert:

                      _____

- **admit**   To send toward (allow): _____

- **emissary**   A person sent outside his country to accomplish good will can be called
  e: outside   a(n) _____ of good will.
  mis: send

- **sent together**   A police commission is literally a group of people
                      "_____" to accomplish some task.

- **premise**   A statement or generalization "sent before" and assumed to be true is
                      a(n) _____. Here are examples of premises used in a
                      syllogism, a type of reasoning chain you studied earlier:
                          Major premise: Misbehaving children should be scolded.
                          Minor premise: Dennis is a misbehaving child.
                          Conclusion: Dennis should be scolded.

- **missile**   The suffix *-ile* means "that which." Nowadays a self-propelled bomb
                      or rocket is called a(n) _____. (that which is sent
                      through the air)

- **sent**   Although the use is no longer current, a letter can be called a *missive*—
                      "something _____."

- **he yields ("lets go   *Miss* can sometimes have the meaning "let go." What do we mean if
  under") to the   we say that a husband is *submissive?* _____
  authority or
  control of his wife**

- **the pain left him   For reasons that were not clear to his doctors, Howard enjoyed a
  temporarily**   remission of the arthritic pain that plagued him. What does *remission*
                        mean in this context? _____

- **sending out   An efficient smog-control device will cut down the emission of pollu-
  pollutants**   tants from gasoline motors. What does *emission* mean in this context?

                      _____

SELF-TEST   1. The former president was the country's most successful emissary to
                 political hot spots around world. What is an emissary?

                 _____

2. I agree with your major _____ that children from broken homes are often troubled, but not with your conclusion that they should be put in orphanages. (generalization assumed to be true.)

3. A ban on carrying "boom boxes" greatly cut down on the _____ of noise. (sending out)

4. The examining team at the hospital said not to expect any remission of Clara's illness. *Remission* means _____.

5. Please enclose the _____ of your delinquent mortgage installments or we will foreclose on your house. (payment)

6. _____ children are not necessarily the "best" children; they may be repressed emotionally. (yielding to the authority or control of someone else)

7. Members of the Congressional _____ failed to agree on a new educational policy. (group "sent together" to handle a particular task)

8. A clergyman sends out a *missive* to the members of his congregation. What would we call a missive today? _____

9. What do we call something "sent" through the air, such as a rocket or bomb? _____

ANSWERS   1. a person sent out of his or her country to accomplish good will 2. premise 3. emission 4. temporary going away 5. remittance 6. submissive 7. commission 8. a letter 9. a missile

24   PENS, PEND, POND: hang, weigh

Prefixes	Suffixes
ap: on	*ant:* that which
com: with, together	*ant:* one who
de: down, from	*ary:* place of
ex: out	*ous:* marked by
im: over	
re: again, back	

Derivatives   appendage (uh PEN dij)
appendix (uh PEN diks)
compensation (kom pen SAY shun)
dependent (dee PEN dunt)
dispensary (dis PEN sir ee)

dispense (dis PENCE)
expend (eks PEND)
impend (im PEND)
pendant (PEN dunt)
pendulum (PEN juh lum)
pensive (PEN sive)
ponderous (PON der ous)
recompense (REK um penss)

• **weigh out**
ex: out
pend: weigh

The words derived from this root were associated originally with the process of *weighing* out money or some form of currency on scales (the old-fashioned kind, with two pans opposite each other *hanging* from a point of balance, as the "scales of justice" are usually pictured). Thus, to expend money is to "_____" money—that is, spend it.

• **weigh together**
com: together
pens: weigh

If you give someone *compensation* for the work he has done you, you "_____" the work and the money owed him, so the work and money will balance each other in the scale.

• **payment**

Compensation is thus: a gift/payment.

• **paid back**

If you do something for someone else without thought of *recompense*, you do it without expecting to be: appreciated/paid back.

• **something that hangs from a chain or wire**

What kind of ornament is a *pendant*? _____

• **"one that hangs from"; one who relies on another for support**

Visualize a baby or small child in its mother's arms and you will see why it is called a dependent. A *dependent* is _____.

• **"that which hangs on"; an addition**

Occasionally the prefix *ap-* means "on." An appendix at the end of a book is what? _____

• **something hanging on to the body**

An arm or leg is technically an appendage. What visual image does *appendage* bring to mind? _____

• **awaiting action**

A new environmental control act is *pending* in Congress. It is: awaiting action/causing controversy.

- **a storm that is about to occur**
  im: over
  pend: hang

What is an *impending* storm? _____

- **dispensary**

People who *dispense* (give out) medicines or medical advice for free or for a small charge work in a place (*-ary*) called a(n) _____.

- **pond**

A person with Lou Gehrig's disease may walk *ponderously*. Which syllable indicates the condition creates the appearance of walking under a heavy burden? _____

- **ponderous**

A book or discussion that is dull and tiresome is also _____. (weighty)

- **weighing a decision**

If you are pondering what to do next, what are you doing? _____

- **weighing**

Rachel is in a pensive mood. She is _____ some sad or sober ideas.

- **heavy**

In a long-running TV series, the Cartwright family owned a big ranch in Nevada called the *Ponderosa*. The ranch got its name from the many *ponderosa* pine trees that grew there. *Ponderosa* pines are literally "_____ pines."

SELF-TEST

1. No _____ is sufficient for the job I have to do. (Payment—two words are appropriate here)

2. The elephants began their _____ trek across the Serengeti. (heavy; slow and unwieldy)

3. She is in a *pensive* frame of mind and not much fun to be with. Pensive means _____.

4. What she called a(n) _____ was no more than an uneven piece of rock suspended from a leather thong. (hanging ornament)

5. The Coast Guard warned small boats of impending danger. *Impending* means _____.

6. A bill authorizing the state to purchase more land for recreation is still pending. What does *pending* mean? _____

7. A person's limbs can be thought of as _____ to his or her body. (parts hanging on to the body)

8. The supplemental material usually attached to the end of a piece of writing, such as a book, is called a(n) _____.

1. recompense or compensation 2. ponderous 3. weighing sad or sober thoughts; reflective 4. pendant 5. about to happen; "hanging over" 6. awaiting action; hanging 7. appendages 8. appendix

25   PLIC, PLI, PLY: fold, bend

Prefixes
com: with, together
ex: out
im: in, within
re: again, back
du: two
multi: many
tri: three

Suffixes
ance: act of
ant: relating to
ate: verb ending
ation: act of, state of
it: marked by
ity: act of, state of

Derivatives
compliance (kum PLEYE unce)
complicate (KOM plih kate)
complication (kom plih KAY shun)
complicity (kum PLISS ih tee)
duplicity (due PLISS ih tee)
explicit (ek SPLISS it)
implicit (im PLISS it)
multiplicity (mull tih PLISS uh tee)
pliant (PLEYE unt)
replica (REP lih kuh)
triplicate (TRIP lih cut)

• **folds**
tri: three
plic: fold

A letter typed in *triplicate* makes three _____ or copies, but the word is commonly used to mean the original plus two copies.

- a copy or reproduction

Replica means "that which is folded again." A *replica* of a famous building in Europe would be: a copy or reproduction/something without similarities to anything else.

- **complicate**
  com: together
  plic: fold

- **a confused state of affairs**

If you "fold your life together," you mix it up or _____ it. Almost nobody gets by without a little complication in his or her life. What does *complication* mean in this context?

_____

- **many folds**
  multi: many
  ply: fold

- **There are such a great variety of things to enjoy.**

Multiply literally means "_____." To *multiply* your chances for success means to make many "folds" or increases. A retired man says, "There are such a *multiplicity* of things to enjoy, I can't imagine ever becoming bored." What does he mean?

_____

- **double-dealing or deceitfulness**

A friend accuses Tom of *duplicity*. If *du* means "double," what is Tom accused of? _____

- **folded together**
- **a partner in crime**

Complicity literally means "_____." If a person is charged with *complicity* in a crime, she is: a partner in crime/an innocent bystander.

- **readily influenced ("bent") by others**

How would you characterize a *pliant* person? _____

- **yield to**

A sergeant has the *compliance* of his men in performing a task. They: resist/yield to him.

- **explicit**

The boss's orders are _____; they are clearly stated. ("folded out"; unfolded)

- **implicit**

If someone's opinion of you is not clearly stated but implied ("folded in"), that opinion is _____.

SELF-TEST

1. The attorney general charged him with complicity in the murder of the union leader. *Complicity* means _____.

2. They got lost because Harry's instructions were not _____ enough. (clearly stated; "folded out")

3. The interior of their house was said to be a(n) _____ of 10 Downing Street. (copy; something "folded again")

4. When she began dating again after her divorce, she decided that she preferred a(n) _____ of shallow relationships to a single deep one with a shallow man. (a great number of choices; "many folds")

5. We forwarded the letter to Mr. Furness in *compliance* with your request. That is, the letter was forwarded: in addition to your request/as you requested/contrary to your request.

6. Lady Margaret rebuked him sharply. "Your guilt is implicit in your manner of speaking about the young lady." *Implicit* means _____.

7. At that age most children are quite _____. (easily molded; readily influenced)

8. A single signature on the credit card receipt created a record in _____ for the customer, the restaurant, and the bank. (an original and two copies; "three folds")

9. After the firm went bankrupt, Bert was shattered to find that it had been caused by his partner's *duplicity.* What does *duplicity* mean? _____

ANSWERS   1. involvement; being "folded together" 2. explicit 3. replica 4. multiplicity 5. as you requested 6. not clearly stated but implied; "folded in" 7. pliant 8. triplicate 9. double-dealing; deceitfulness

26   SCRIB, SCRIPT: write

Prefixes	Suffixes
a: to, toward	*ion:* act of
circum: around	
con: together, with	
de: down	
non: not	
pre: before	
pro: forward, in front of, in favor of	
sub: under, below	

Derivatives	ascribe (uh SKRIBE)
	circumscribe (SIR kum skribe)
	conscription (kun SKRIP shun)
	describe (duh SKRIBE)
	nondescript (NON duh SKRIPT)
	prescribe (pruh SKRIBE)
	proscribe (pro SKRIBE)
	scribble (SKRIB uhl)
	subscribe (sub SKRIBE)

- **scribbles**

If you write a note quickly and carelessly, your handwriting may look like _____ .

- **write down**
  de: down
  scrib: write

To *describe* yourself you would "_____" your most distinctive features—those things that make you different from others.

- **is not**

A *nondescript* person (is/is not) very different or unique.

- **under**

Tamara *subscribes* to public radio. She "_____ writes" it or supports it with her money. Explain what *subscribe* means in this sentence: Newton *subscribes* to the president's theories on

- **He supports the idea**

workfare. _____

- **limited**

Our vacation this year will be *circumscribed* by a lack of money. It will be "written around" by money and will thus be: limited/avoided.

- **circumscribe**

The Queen tried to restrict or _____ her daughter-in-law's social activities. ("write around")

- **write toward**
  a: toward
  scrib: write

Several reputable critics have *ascribed* the painting to Leonardo da Vinci. That means they have said he: did/did not paint it. Your answer is proved by the literal meaning of *ascribe:* to "_____ ."

- **prescribed**

Medicines are *prescribed* by doctors. Certain dangerous or unlawful acts are *proscribed* (forbidden) by those in authority. The antibiotic was _____ by Doctor Bailey. Black-market trading was

- **proscribed**

_____ by the Commanding Officer.

• conscription

Occasionally the prefix *con-* means "down." What is the term identifying the process whereby the law compels young men of military age to be enrolled ("written down") in the military service?

_____

SELF-TEST

1. Safety officers _____ the decrease in highway fatalities to the lowered speed limits. (assign; "write toward")

2. Legal problems greatly *circumscribed* his television appearances. That is, his appearances were _____.

3. Many people feel that smoking in public buildings and public transportation services should be proscribed. *Proscribed* means: forbidden/encouraged/surveyed.

4. Eunice has always _____ to the idea that hard work and responsibility make life interesting and worthwhile. (supported; underwritten)

5. The General has always believed in the universal _____ of men for the armed forces. (enrollment)

6. The agent's nondescript appearance was a great advantage in covert operations for the CIA. What does *nondescript* mean?

_____

ANSWERS

1. ascribe 2. limited; restricted; "written around" 3. forbidden 4. subscribed 5. conscription 6. not different or unique

27   SED, SID, SESS: sit, settle

Prefixes	Suffixes
as: to, toward	*al:* marked by
re: again, back	*ary:* marked by
sub: under, below	*ary:* that which
super: above, beyond, over	*ate:* marked by
	ive: that which
	ment: that which
	ous: marked by

	Derivatives	assiduous (uh SID jew us)

Derivatives
- assiduous (uh SID jew us)
- reside (ree ZIDE)
- residual (ree ZID jew uhl)
- sedate (suh DATE)
- sedative (SED uh tiv)
- sedentary (SED un tare ee)
- sediment (SED ih munt)
- subsidiary (sub SID ee air ee)
- subsidy (SUB suh dee)
- supersede (soo per SEED)

- **sitting** — *Sedentary* occupations involve a great deal of _____.

- **replace** — Word processors have *superseded* typewriters. Literally, word processors "sit above" typewriters now in importance. A synonym for supersede would be replace/parallel.

- **calm** — Queen Victoria was often described as a *sedate* woman. She did sit at court a great deal, no doubt, but the adjective means that she was: calm and dignified/excitable.

- **sedative** — To settle someone's nerves or calm him down a doctor often prescribes a(n) _____. (-*ive* = that which)

- **the substance that settles to the bottom** — As a bottle of wine matures, *sediment* is formed in the bottom of the bottle. What is *sediment*? _____

- **residual**
  re: back
  sid: sit
  — A *residue* is something left over, something that settles back. Things made from leftovers are _____ products. (of or pertaining to residue)

- **He "sits toward" his work busily and attentively.**
  as: toward
  sid: sit
  — How would you characterize an *assiduous* worker? _____

- **having a meeting, sitting** — If Congress or some similar group is in *session*, what is it doing? _____

- **subside**

When storms, strong emotions, or fast-paced activities lessen in intensity, they are said to _____. ("sit under")

- **assists or supplements**

A large company has the controlling interest in two smaller companies that it designates as its *subsidiaries*. A *subsidiary*: assists or supplements/competes against the main company.

Literally a *subsidy* was once "reserve troops," initially coming from the idea of extra soldiers who sat near the action at hand.

- **subsidy**

When a government or business provides money to an enterprise that can't support itself, that aid is called a(n) _____.

SELF-TEST

1. Eleanor sat opposite the judge and his wife, looking queenly and _____. (calm and dignified)

2. The new trade pact required reductions in farm subsidies. What is a subsidy? _____

3. Mr. Fullerton commended Pauline for the *assiduous* way in which she kept the accounts up to date. Fullerton was: praising Pauline's work/telling Pauline the accounts were badly handled/laughing at Pauline for bothering with accounts.

4. The doctor warned that leading too _____ a life could seriously damage the heart. (marked by sitting)

5. They could not leave the cave until the storm subsided. *Subsided* means _____.

6. After the flood the ground floor of the house was covered with a four-inch layer of _____ or _____.

7. Mildred was still unable to calm down after taking a(n) _____. (drug used to settle nerves)

8. The star of a TV series often signs a contract that allows him residual payments if the series is used as a rerun. What does *residual* mean? _____

9. A company that operates independently but is under the control of another company is called a(n) _____.

ANSWERS

1. sedate 2. assistance given to a person or business 3. praising Pauline's work
4. sedentary 5. lessened in intensity; "settled under" 6. sediment or residue 7. sedative
8. leftover or additional; "marked by settling back" 9. subsidiary

28 SENT, SENS: feel

Prefixes	Suffixes
dis: apart, not	*al:* characterized by
pre: before	*ion:* act of, state of
	ity: state of
	ment: state of
	ory: characterized by
	ous: characterized by

Derivatives

dissension (dih SEN shun)
dissent (dih SENT)
presentiment (pre ZENT ih munt)
sensory (SENSE er ee)
sensual (SENSE yoo uhl)
sensuous (SEN shoo us)
sentiment (SENT uh munt)
sentimentality (sent ih men TAL uh tee)

• **sensory**

An impression that affects your ability to see, hear, taste, touch, and smell is a(n) _____ impression. *Sensual* and *sensuous* are adjectives that pertain to the bodily senses, but are used in different ways. *Sensuous* most commonly means enjoying the pleasures of the senses: a *sensuous* love of colors and textures, the *sensuous* comfort of a warm bed on a cold night. *Sensual*, on the other hand, commonly implies a criticism—caring too much for the pleasures of the body, putting them ahead of the mind or soul: a man of a low, *sensual* nature; a book filled with *sensual* overtones. Distinguish these words in the following sentences. The prophet warned him to put aside such

• **sensual**
• **sensuous**

_____ desires. She delighted in the _____ thrill of running her hands over the expensive furs.

• **feeling beforehand**

A *presentiment* of danger is a: feeling beforehand/unrecognized feeling that something bad is about to happen.

• **sentiment**

Sentiment is a feeling, especially of a tender or refined kind: the *sentiment* expressed by a mother for her baby. *Sentimentality*, on the other hand, is a gushy, over-emotional expression of feeling that does not seem quite justified: the *sentimentality* of a drunk who cries and keeps telling everyone how much he loves his wife. When people are *sentimental*, they

• **sentimentality**

usually exaggerate their feelings—and enjoy doing so. (Who hasn't taken a *sentimental* journey down memory lane?) So a justifiable tender feeling is _____, while an exaggerated, gushy, over-emotional feeling is _____.

The proposal to build the new factory caused *dissension* between those who wanted to create more jobs and those who were worried about pollution.

• **quarreling**
dis: apart
sens: feeling

Dissension means: agreement/quarreling.

• **dissension**

• **dissent**

Whereas *dissension* means a hard feeling caused by differences of opinion, the word *dissent* is the actual difference of opinion or the right to differ from prevailing opinion: Political *dissent* is a part of the American system. To review: quarreling and the bad feeling brought on by differences of opinion is called _____; a difference of opinion is called _____.

SELF-TEST

1. The perfume of the apple blossoms was one of the _____ delights of May in Normandy. (marked by enjoying the pleasures of the senses)

2. I couldn't see, but noise, texture, taste, and other _____ impressions seemed more vivid. (relating to the ability to see, hear, touch, taste, and smell)

3. He was too devoted to gratification of his sensual needs to be a very dependable friend. *Sensual* means _____.

4. Polly resigned as president of the women's bridge club, saying she felt her recent actions were responsible for the bitter dissension. What does *dissension* mean? _____

5. Is a *dissenting* judge for a majority opinion or against it? _____

6. The poem is a moving depiction of the _____ he felt upon first hearing of the birth of his son. (justifiable tender feeling)

7. Ms. Langtry was realistic and matter-of-fact, and she thought anyone who would waste tears on a dilapidated old cabin in the hills was guilty of foolishness or _____ or both. (exaggerated emotional feeling)

8. Acting on his _____, the supervisor ordered the workers out of the structure just minutes before it collapsed. ("feeling beforehand")

1. sensuous 2. sensory 3. devoting too much time to the pleasure of the senses 4. quarreling or hard feeling about differences of opinion 5. against it 6. sentiment 7. sentimentality 8. presentiment

29 SPEC, SPIC: look, see

Prefixes

as (ad): to, toward
circum: around
in: in, into
intro: within
per: complete, thorough
pro: forward, in front of, in favor of
retro: backward

Suffixes

ion: act of
ive: that which
re: that which
rum: that which

Derivatives

aspect (ASS spekt)
circumspect (SIR kum spekt)
inspect (in SPEKT)
introspection (in tro SPEK shun)
perspective (per SPEK tiv)
prospect (PRAH spekt)
retrospect (REH truh spekt)
spectacles (SPEK tuh kuhls)
specter (SPEK ter)
spectrum (SPEK trum)

- **inspects**
  in: in
  spect: look

She always _____ my room first. (looks in)

- **the act of looking backward**
  retro: backward
  spect: look

He sat in his cell for hours regretting his life in retrospect. What does *retrospect* mean? _____

• **act of looking within**
  intro: within
  spect: look

Imprisonment had forced him into serious introspection, and he vowed to change himself for the better. What does *introspection* mean?
_____

• **circumspect**

Tim is usually _____ in his choice of friends. ("marked by looking around")

• **perspective**

It would help you understand this problem if you would look at it from the _____ of a psychologist. (viewpoint; complete look)

• **prospect**

We are faced with the _____ of higher prices. ("look forward")

• **aspects**
  a: toward
  spec: look

There are many _____ of the problem to consider. ("ways of looking toward")

• **eyeglasses**

Granny left her spectacles on the wash basin. *Spectacles* are: eyeglasses/false teeth/bracelets.

• **looked**

Rugs available in a full *spectrum* of colors are available in a wide range of things to be _____ at or seen.

• **specter**

A *specter* is a ghost, a thing seen in the mind. The Western world is still haunted by the _____ of falling living standards.

SELF-TEST

1. The Higbys were totally unaware of the legal _____ of the matter. ("ways of looking toward")

2. In _____ the trip seemed much more pleasurable than it had actually been. (act of looking backward)

3. He was sorely tormented by the specter of his guilt. What does *specter* mean? _____

4. Freedom should give one the fullest spectrum of choice possible. A *spectrum* refers to _____.

5. His answers to the detective's questions were always polite, always _____. (marked by looking around; careful)

6. Thrilled by the _____ of a fishing trip with his dad, Larry got out of bed the minute he was awakened. ("look forward")

7. You are not looking at your problems from the right perspective. What does *perspective* mean? _____

8. The long illness forced her into some painful but necessary introspection. *Introspection* is the act of _____.

1. aspects 2. retrospect 3. something seen in the mind 4. the entire range of something 5. circumspect 6. prospect 7. viewpoint; complete look at something 8. looking within

30   SOLV, SOLUT: free, loosen

Prefixes   **Suffixes**
ab: from, away   *ion:* act of
dis: apart, not   *ent:* being
in: not
re: again, back

Derivatives   absolute (AB suh lute)
absolution (ab suh LEW shun)
absolve (ab ZOLV)
dissolute (DIS suh lute)
dissolution (dis suh LEW shun)
dissolve (dih ZOLV)
insolvent (in SOL vunt)
resolution (rez uh LEW shun)
resolve (ree ZOLV)
solvent (SOL vunt)

• **solvent**
solve: free
ent: being

A business that is free of debt or that can pay its debts readily is _____. (being free)

• **insolvent**

If you are temporarily out of money, you can say—euphemistically—that you are _____. (not free)

• **brought to an end**
dis: apart
solv: free

A relationship that is *dissolved* is: _____.

- **dissolute**
People who are loose in morals or conduct are said to be
_____. ("loosened apart")

- **dissolution**
Overindulgence in food, drink, and the like is called
_____. (act of loosening apart)

- **free from**
  ab: from
  solv: free
- **absolution**

A man is absolved of guilt feelings by confessing his sins to a priest.
Absolve means to _____. Upon his confession, the
priest gives the man _____. (the act of freeing from)

- **free from**
If you have *absolute* authority or power, you are: under/free from the
influence or control of someone else.

- **you determine to
get one**

Resolve literally means "free again," usually to free yourself from
doubt. If you *resolve* to get a college education, what do you do?

_____

- **resolution**
When an organization determines to do some special thing, such as trying to save an old landmark from the bulldozer, it puts its determination on record by passing a(n) _____.

SELF-TEST

1. He entered the little church, seeking absolution for his evil thoughts
and deeds. What is *absolution*? _____

2. After years of incredible popularity, Elvis fell into a life of *dissolution.*
Dissolution means _____

3. The firm is _____ and will soon go bankrupt. (not
free from debt)

4. After the military takeover, Diego was made head of the provisional
government and given _____ power. He quickly
made himself into a dictator. (free from the influence or control of someone else)

5. The conservation club quickly passed a(n) _____ to
request the governor to withhold his endorsement of the proposed
new dam. (determination)

6. After the accident in which her friend was killed, she was never to
feel _____ of guilt. (freed from)

ANSWERS

1. forgiveness; act of being freed from guilt 2. loose in morals or conduct; "loosening
apart" 3. insolvent 4. absolute 5. resolution 6. absolved

31   SPIR: breathe

Prefixes

as (ad): to, toward
con: with, together
dis: apart, not
ex: out
in: in
per: through,
  thoroughly
re: again, back

Suffixes

ation: act of

Derivatives   aspire (uh SPIRE)
conspire (kun SPIRE)
dispirited (dis SPIR uh tuhd)
expire (ik SPIRE)
inspire (in SPIRE)
perspire (per SPIRE)
respiration (res per AY shun)
spirited (SPIR uh tuhd)
spirometer (spir OM uh ter)

- **"breathe out"**
  ex: out
  spire: breathe

Expire literally means to _____.

- **expire**

Often *expire* means to breathe out for the last time, or die. If a license of some sort is about to run out, it, too, is said to _____.

- **inspire**
  in: in
  spir: breathe

To "breathe" courage into someone is to _____ courage.

- **conspire**
  con: together
  spir: breathe

Think of people "breathing together" in dark corners to plot evil or harm against somebody else and you will have a vivid reference for the verb _____.

- **earnestly desired**

Aspire means "breathe toward." Bill Clinton *aspired* to be president. Here *aspired* means: gave up trying/earnestly desired.

- **inhaling and exhaling air**

A doctor measures your rate of *respiration*, which means your rate of: giving off moisture/inhaling and exhaling air.

• perspire

To "breathe through" the skin is to _____.

• lively

"Breath" and "life" are almost synonymous for human beings, so a *spirited* discussion would be: lively/unnecessary.

• lacking spirit; discouraged

A setback or defeat of some kind leaves most people feeling dispirited. What does *dispirited* mean? _____

• breathing; lung capacity

A *spirometer* is an instrument for measuring what?
_____

SELF-TEST

1. This contract and its provisions will *expire* in six months. That is, in six months the contract will: begin/be reactivated/die.

2. Most people in the United States think that several groups _____ to assassinate President Kennedy. ("breathed together")

3. Secretly, he aspired to be president of the country. *Aspired* means _____.

4. When sales continued to drop over an eight-week period, even the most optimistic merchants became _____. (discouraged)

5. They were having a spirited conversation about the merits of domestic cars versus foreign cars. *Spirited* means _____.

6. The effects of emphysema were checked by weekly tests made by using a(n) _____. (instrument for measuring lung capacity)

7. If we say that a patient's *respiration* is irregular, what do we mean? _____

ANSWERS   1. die 2. conspired 3. desired or hoped; "breathed toward" 4. dispirited 5. lively
6. spirometer 7. that her rate of inhaling and exhaling is irregular

32   **TEMPOR: time**

Prefixes	Suffixes
con: with, together	al: that which
ex: out of, outside	ary: one who
pro: in favor of	ary: one who
	ary: relating to
	eous: characterized by being
	ize: verb ending

Derivatives	contemporaneous (kun temp er AY nee us)
	contemporary (kun TEMP er air ee)
	extemporaneous (eks temp er AY nee us)
	pro tem (PRO TEM)
	temporal (TEM poe ruhl)
	temporary (TEM per air ee)
	tempo (TEM poe)
	temporize (TEM per ize)

- **time**
  tempor: time
  ary: relating to

A *temporary* job lasts for only a limited _____.

- **time**

If you *temporize* about a decision, you delay in making it; you use up _____ in discussion.

- **not having time to prepare ahead; speaking "off the cuff" as you go along**

The literal meaning of *extemporaneous* is "being out of time." Give a more current definition of it as it occurs in the following sentence: The president spoke well from a script, but when he gave an *extemporaneous* speech, he often made a fool of himself.

_____

- **together in time**
  con: together
  tempor: time
  ary: one who

You and the people of your age are contemporaries. *Contemporaries* literally means those "_____."

- **were not**

- **contemporary**

George Washington and John Kennedy: were/were not contemporaries. Authors presently living or alive in the past twenty or thirty years would be included in a course in _____ literature. ("together in time" with you)

- **yes**

If they are held in the same period of time, would a horse show and a music festival be *contemporaneous* events? _____

- **acting; someone who serves "for the time being"**

If *pro* means "for," what is a chairman *pro tem*?

_____

- **the time or rate of movement of the music; the rhythm**

An orchestra leader plays a well-known composition at a much faster tempo than usual. What do you think *tempo* means in this context?

_____

SELF-TEST

1. In the early days of his administration President Lincoln was not highly regarded by many of his _____. (those of approximately the same age; those "together in time")

2. Three times Sir Gawain asked the king to send help to the Gauls, and three times the king temporized. What does *temporized* mean?
_____

3. While the vice president is away on a trip, the majority leader is president *pro tem* of the Senate. *Pro tem* means _____.

4. In some rural areas the _____ of life is still leisurely and graceful. (time; rhythm)

5. The public relations staff worries every time their chairman makes *extemporaneous* remarks. Why do they worry? _____

6. My son's hockey game and my daughter's dance recital are *contemporaneous* events. Can I go to both? _____

ANSWERS

1. contemporaries 2. stalled for time; engaged in pointless discussion 3. for the time being 4. tempo 5. Because he hasn't taken time to prepare and might say something that would lead to trouble 6. no, they're in the same period of time

33 TORT: twist

Prefixes

con: with, together
dis: apart, not
ex: out
re: again, back

Suffixes

ion: act of
ist: one who
ous: marked by
ure: act of

Derivatives

contortion (kun TOR shun)
contortionist (kun TOR shun ist)
distort (dis TORT)
extort (eks TORT)
extortion (eks TOR shun)
retort (ree TORT)
tortuous (TOR chew us)
torture (TOR chure)
torturous (TOR cher us)

- **by twisting it out of shape**
  tort: twist
  ure: act of

During the Middle Ages confessions were often obtained through *torture*, such as putting a man on the rack. How was pain inflicted on the body? _____

- **distort**

It is usually unwise to _____ the truth. ("twist apart")

- **to reply sharply; to return in kind**

Retort means "to twist back." Give the current meaning in this sentence: "You're just as lazy as I am!" she *retorted.* _____

- **twisting the body parts together**
  con: together
  tort: twist
  ion: act of

Gene went through all kind of contortions as he tried to get through the tiny open window. What does *contortion* mean? _____

- **contortionist**

A person who entertains others by unusual or difficult "twistings" of the body is called a(n) _____.

- **twist out**
  ex: out
  tort: twist

Criminals often try to extort money from people. *Extort* literally means to "_____."

- **extortion**

There are laws against such acts of _____.

- **torturous**

Two adjectives sharing the root *tort* are sometimes confused. A *tortuous* road is full of twists and turns; a *torturous* illness is cruelly painful. Building the pyramids was _____ work for the slaves. The winding path up the hill is _____.

- **tortuous**

SELF-TEST

1. After the subway fire, the police uncovered evidence of a plan to *extort* money from the city. What does *extort* mean? _____

2. It was _____ work having to pull the sled by hand. (cruelly painful)

3. Even wild sheep would have had trouble following that _____ mountain path. (twisting; winding)

4. We could tell he was suffering by the _____ of his face. (twistings together; grimaces)

5. "My mother may be limited, as you say, but at least she doesn't brag about her ignorance!" Liz _____. (replied quickly or sharply; returned in kind)

1. to "twist out"; demand 2. torturous 3. tortuous 4. contortions 5. retorted

34 VID, VIS: see, look

Prefixes

ad: to, toward
im: not
in: not
pro: forward, in front of, in favor of
re: again, back
super: over

Suffixes

ence: act of
er: one who
ation: act of
ally: adverb; manner

Derivatives   advise (ad VIZE)
improvisation (im prahv uh ZAY shun)
improvise (IM pro vize)
improviser (IM pruh vize er)
invidious (in VID ee us)
providence (PRAHV uh dunss)
providentially (prahv uh DEN shul lee)
revise (ree VIZE)
supervise (SOO per vize)

• **You "look toward" his problem.**
ad: toward
vise: look

What do you do when you *advise* someone? _____

• **look again**
re: again
vise: look

If you *revise* your opinion about something, you "_____."

- **overlook workers to see they do their work properly**
  super: over
  vis: look
  or: one who

Keeping in mind the literal meaning, what is a *supervisor's* general function? To _____.

- **the act of seeing forward (ahead)**
  pro: forward
  vid: see
  ence: act of

A religious person often feels that God has taken an active role in causing things to happen: It was divine providence that the rain came just in time to save the crops. What does *providence* mean here literally? _____

- **providentially**

If you feel something happens to you at just the right time, you can say that it happened _____. (in the manner of providence)

- **improvisation**

A teacher is caught without time to prepare a test, so when he arrives in class he has to *improvise:* that is, to make one up as he goes along. Literally, to *improvise* means to do something "not seeing forward (without looking ahead of time)." Music that is made up as the performer goes along is called _____. Most jazz musi-

- **improvisers**

cians are good _____.

- **invidious**

Invidious literally means "not seeing." An *invidious* remark is unfair or offensive. If you were to be compared with an especially talented or good-looking brother or sister, no doubt you would feel the comparison to be _____.

SELF-TEST

1. Aid from the state arrived _____ every year, allowing the city to balance its budget, but with the economy in a recession, the city was forced to raise taxes instead. (just at the right time; in the manner of divine intervention)

2. Ruth forgot her lines, but the ones she _____ got a bigger laugh than the ones the playwright had written. (made up lines "without looking" ahead)

3. Jeanne felt it was _____ to compare her with a woman twice her age. (unfair or offensive; "not seeing")

4. If you are a good enough musician to call yourself an *improviser,* what are you able to do? _____

1. providentially 2. improvised 3. invidious 4. to make up music as you play it

35   VOC, VOCAT, VOK: call, calling

Prefixes	Other Roots	Suffixes
ad: to, toward	*equi:* equal	*ate:* one who
a: not		*ation:* act of
con: with, together		*able:* able
e: out of		*ative:* that which
in: on		
ir: not		
pro: forward, forth		
re: again, back		

Derivatives   advocate (AD vuh kut)
advocation (av oh KAY shun)
convocation (kon voh KAY shun)
equivocate (ee QUIV oh kate)
evoke (ee VOKE)
invoke (in VOKE)
irrevocable (ir REV uh kuh buhl)
provoke (pruh VOKE)
revoke (ree VOKE)
vocal (VOE kuhl)
vocation (voe KAY shun)

- **by speaking**   A vocal protest is made: by speaking/in writing.

- **revoked**   A drunk driver may have his driver's license _____.
  re: back   (called back)
  vok: call

- **irrevocable**   An action or decision that can never be "called back" is
  _____.

- **to call it forth**   What does it mean to *provoke* a response from a friend?
  pro: forward   _____
  vok: call

- **They call on the gods to send rain.**

In a special ceremony the Hopi Indians *invoke* the gods to send rain. What do they do? _____

- **recommends**
  ad: toward
  voc: call
  ate: one who

Mr. Cortines is an *advocate* of a longer year for public school students. This means that he: recommends/objects to keeping the schools open in the summer.

- **equivocate**

Mr. Sutton has no firm standards for the firm's public relations program and goes back and forth every time he is consulted about what to put in the annual report. The verb that means to "put equal emphasis in opposed directions" is _____.

- **calling**

A synonym for *vocation* is "_____."

- **avocation**

What someone does with his leisure time is his hobby, or _____. ("not the calling")

- **convocation**

In college a calling together of students is usually called a(n) _____ rather than an assembly.

- **evoke**

The songs in the movie "The Big Chill" _____ a certain era in American life. (call out)

- **that which calls out**

The audience found her artistic theories so *provocative* that they argued with her from the audience. What does *provocative* mean?
_____

SELF-TEST

1. His action seemed as irrevocable as dropping a letter into a mailbox. What does *irrevocable* mean? _____

2. The preacher *invoked* the name of the Almighty to help him combat charges of embezzlement, but eventually his congregation fired him. *Invoked* means to _____.

3. Voters were irritated by the president's tendency to _____ over almost every policy and every appointment, although he argued that there were no simple answers to complex questions. (speak with equal emphasis in opposite directions)

4. Although I make my living by raising greenhouse plants, my _____ is playing a jazz saxophone.

5. Professor Greene is an advocate of free trade. What is an *advocate?*
   _____

6. The new student body regulations will be discussed in a(n)
   _____ to be held at eleven o'clock this morning.
   (meeting; assembly)

7. The Motor Vehicle Bureau threatened to revoke my driver's license.
   What does *revoke* mean? _____

8. My seven-year old daughter does the opposite of what I ask to *pro-voke* me. What does *provoke* mean? _____

ANSWERS   1. not able to be recalled 2. "called on" 3. equivocate 4. avocation 5. a supporter; one who "calls toward" 6. convocation 7. "to call back" 8. "to call forth"

Now that you've mastered this chapter, you might enjoy a new look at the drawing that opens it on page 82.

ANTEHILL

SUBSMASH

INTERDISHES

PRETYPEWRITER

5 Latin Prefixes

AB-, ABS-: from, away

Roots
duct: lead
err: wander
rad: root
solve: free, loosen
tain, tin: hold

Suffixes
ant: marked by
ence: act of
ion: act of

Derivatives   abduct (ab DUKT)
aberrant (AB er unt)
abnormal (ab NOR muhl)
aborigine (ab er IJ juhn ee)
abrade (uh BRADE)
absolution (ab so LOO shun)
absolve (ab ZOLVE)
abstain (ab STAIN)
abstinence (AB stin unce)

• **abnormal**	If your temperature is much higher or lower than *normal*, it is _____.
• **led away** *ab:* away *duct:* lead	A person who is kidnapped is *abducted,* which literally means "_____."
• **from**	*Aborigines* are people who have maintained the same tribal identity _____ the beginning (origin).
• **He has been freed from guilt.**	In the course of an investigation, a man has been *absolved* of guilt. What has been done to him? _____
• **freedom from guilt (forgiveness)**	In some religions a person who confesses her sins is given *absolution.* What is she given? _____
• **aberrant**	What adjective describes the behavior of a man who wanders from the right or usual path? _____ behavior
• **speaks away** *ab:* away *dic:* speak	An aging king decides to *abdicate.* He gives up his throne or authority. Literally he "_____" his authority, usually in a public ceremony.
• **to their roots**	The walls of a canyon are gradually abraded by dust storms and muddy water. How deep are they worn?
• **hold away from it**	If you *abstain* from some activity, such as smoking or drinking, you: participate in it/hold away from it.
• **abstinence**	Members of a religious order who hold away from sexual activity are said to practice _____. (act of holding away)

SELF-TEST

1. The Australian bushmen, who live today much as men did in the Stone Age, are _____. (from the beginning)

2. Once she had been _____ of blame for the accident, she felt much better. (freed from)

3. The brothers in a religious order must take a vow of _____. (holding away)

4. The instructor forced the frog to ingest some alcohol and then asked us to observe any aberrant patterns of behavior it manifested. *Aberrant* means _____.

5. If the marble exterior of an old building has been badly *abraded,* what has happened to it? _____

1. aborigines 2. absolved 3. abstinence 4. "wandering from" the usual pattern 5. it has been scraped, or worn, away; it has lost its smoothness

2 AD- (af-, ag-, al-, am-, an-, ap-, ar-, as-, at-): to, toward

Roots
grav: serious, worse
loc: place
orare: pray
simil: like
tract: draw
vis: look, see

Suffixes
ate: verb ending
ation: act of
ing: current act of

Derivatives
adjoining (uh JOIN ing)
adore (uh DORE)
aggravate (AG gruh vate)
allocate (AL uh kate)
annotated (AN uh tate uhd)
assimilation (uh sim uh LAY shun)
attract (uh TRAKT)

• **adjoining**

Rooms in a hotel that are literally "joined to" each other are _____ rooms.

• **advises**
ad: toward
vis: look

A faculty advisor who "looks toward" solutions for your problems _____ you.

• **to worship ("pray to") or highly regard him or her**

If *orare* means "pray," what does it mean to *adore* a hero? _____

• **affect**

When *ad-* is added to a root like *range,* the *d* turns into *r: ad + range* becomes *arrange.* (Say *adrange* out loud five or six times as rapidly as possible and you will hear what happens. You will also understand why pronunciation and spelling gradually change over the years.) What does *ad + fect* become? _____ The process whereby the *d* of the prefix *ad-* turns into the same consonant as the one following it is called *assimilation*, "the act of becoming similar to" something else. The word *assimilation* is an example of the very thing it defines: *ad + similation* becomes *assimilation*. Because of the principle of

- **assimilation** _____, the prefix *ad-* sometimes becomes *af-*, *ag-*, *al-*, *am-*, *an-*, *ap-*, *ar-*, or *as-*.

- **attracts**
  at: toward
  tract: draw

  Tract = draw. What does honey do to flies? It _____ them.

- **aggravate it**

  Grave = serious, worse. Scratching may do what to a skin infection? _____

- **allocates**
  al: toward
  loc: place

  Loc = place. The Federal Government _____ _____ a great deal of money for military expenditures.

- **annotated**

  A bibliography containing explanatory *notes* or comments is called a(n) _____ bibliography.

- **assimilation**

  It is interesting to note that *assimilation* also applies to the way in which immigrant people are brought into the mainstream of American culture. They quickly become similar to other Americans, and this process is called _____.

SELF-TEST

1. Each city must _____ a large sum of money for its transportation system. ("place toward")

2. Speaking to your father when you are angry will only aggravate an already tense situation. *Aggravate* means _____.

3. An *annotated* bibliography contains _____.

4. When added to the root *range,* the prefix *ad-* becomes *ar- (arrange).* This process is called _____.

5. If you treat someone as though she were a god—that is, if you worship her—you _____ her.

ANSWERS

1. allocate 2. worsen; make more serious 3. explanatory notes or comments
4. assimilation 5. adore

3   ANTE-: before

Roots	Suffixes
bellum: war	*ent:* one who
cede: go	*ian:* characterized by being
diluv: flood	

Derivatives   antebellum (ant ee BELL um)
antecedents (an tih SEED unts)
antedate (AN tih date)
antediluvian (an tih duh LOO vee un)
anterior (an TEER ee er)
anteroom (AN tee room)

- **before**

Your *antecedents* would be the family members that "go
_____" you; in other words, your ancestors.

- **happened ("dated") before**

World War I *antedated* World War II; that is, it
_____ it.

- **anteroom**

A waiting room that leads to a larger room can also be called a(n)
_____. ("before room")

- **front**

An *anterior* view of something is a: back/front view.

- **Antebellum (used here as a proper noun)**

Bellum means "war." The South before the Civil War is called the
_____ South.

- **before the Flood**

If *diluv* refers to the great Flood (deluge) reported in the Old Testament, what would *antediluvian* mean? _____

- **antediluvian**

If you wish to exaggerate, you can describe something very old as being
_____. (existing before the Flood)

SELF-TEST

1. The famous novel *Gone with the Wind* begins in the Antebellum South. What does *antebellum* mean? _____

2. To nine-year-old Mickey, his father's taste in music seemed
_____. (existing before the great flood; very old)

3. The brain tumor was located in the *anterior* lobe of the brain. Which lobe is that? front/rear/center.

4. My _____ landed at Ellis Island.

5. Lady Margery heard the two ladies chattering away in the _____. (waiting room; "room before")

6. My birthday is in June, while yours is in August; so mine _____ yours by two months. (dates before)

ANSWERS   1. before the war (in this case, the Civil War) 2. antediluvian 3. the front lobe
4. antecedents 5. anteroom 6. antedates

4   **CIRCUM-: around**

Roots
fer: bear, carry
ig: go, carry on
locut: speak
nav: ship
vent: come

Suffixes
ate: verb ending
ence: result of
ion: act of

Derivatives   circumference (sir KUM frince)
circumlocution (sir kum low KEW shun)
circumnavigate (sir kum NAV uh gate)
circumspect (SIR kum spekt)
circumvent (SIR kum vent)

• **around**

The *circumference* of a circle is the line that could be "carried _____" its outer edge.

• **circumnavigate**

Navigate means "to make a ship go." Ferdinand Magellen was the first explorer to _____ the earth. (make a ship go around)

• **circumvent**

To avoid trouble by coming (going) around a problem is to _____ trouble.

- **look around**
  circum: around
  spect: look

If you are *circumspect* in your choice of friends, you
"_____" carefully to act wisely.

- **No**

If you ask a question of a politician and he responds with a *circumlocution*, does he come to the point? _____

- **around**

(He talks all _____ the point.)

SELF-TEST

1. By apologizing to Ed, Martin hoped to _____ further unpleasantness. (go around; avoid)

2. The police were _____ when they questioned Ms. Stern to avoid any hint that she was a suspect. (careful)

3. According to the news writeup, she planned to *circumnavigate* the world in a hot-air balloon. What did she plan to do?
_____

4. After measuring it, Hank said the _____ of the circle was 12.60 feet. (distance around)

5. A person who uses *circumlocutions* is probably trying to: build up interest/avoid an issue.

ANSWERS

1. circumvent 2. circumspect 3. travel around; go around the world 4. circumference
5. avoid an issue

---

5   **COM-, CON-, COL-, CO-: with, together**

Prefix	Roots	Suffixes
in: not	*bin:* bind	*al:* marked by
	gru: agree	*ant:* characterized by being
	jug: yoke	*ate:* verb ending
	plais: please	*ent:* marked by
		ity: state of

Derivatives   collaborate (kuh LAB er ate)
combine (kuhm BINE)

commingle (kum MING uhl)
complaisant (kum PLAY sunt)
congruent (KON grew unt)
conjugal (KON juh guhl)
coordinate (koe ORD in ate)
cooperate (koe OP er ate)
incongruity (in kon GREW uh tee)

- **complaisant**
  com: with
  plais: please
  ant: being

  The prefix *com-* is usually used before roots beginning with *b, p,* or *m.* A person who is obliging or gracious or courteous is a(n) _____ person. ("pleasing with")

- **commingle**

  If many people *mingle* together in a crowd, they are said to _____.

- **combine**

- **together**

  A group of persons joined or bound together for business or political gain is called a(n) _____. As a verb, *combine* means literally "to bind things _____."

- **collaborate**

  The prefix *col-* is used before roots beginning with *l.* Thus, to *labor* with someone else on a project is to _____.

- **cooperate**

  The prefix *co-* is used before roots beginning with *o.* To *operate* together in some fashion is to _____.

- **together**

  If the activities of two groups are *coordinated,* they are regulated _____.

- **yoked together**
  con: together
  jug: yoke

  Most other roots take the prefix *con-.* Being married establishes a *conjugal* relationship between a man and a woman; they are then "_____."

- **conjugal**

  Happy married people refer to their state as _____ bliss.

- **congruent**
  con: with
  gru: agree

  If *gru* means "agree," then two opinions that are harmonious are _____ opinions.

- **that the beliefs and the actions did not agree with each other**

The *incongruity* of a man's stated beliefs and his actions would mean what? _____

SELF-TEST

1. Lester felt lucky indeed; he had married a very complaisant woman. *Complaisant* means _____.

2. Their marriage could hardly be called a state of _____ bliss. (marked by being yoked together)

3. The editorial commented on the *incongruity* of trying to balance the budget while cutting taxes sharply. *Incongruity* means _____.

4. The lawyer _____ funds belonging to different clients in her escrow account, making it difficult to tell whether she was embezzling or not. (mingled together)

5. The Gulf War was a *coordinated* effort by many nations to expel the Iraqi invaders from Kuwait. *Coordinated* means _____.

6. The Attorney General placed the blame for the swindle on a Chicago _____. (group bound together for a business purpose)

7. Although they came from radically different backgrounds, their views on the importance of conservation were _____. (marked by agreeing with each other)

ANSWERS   1. obliging, gracious, "pleasing with" 2. conjugal 3. lack of agreement between two things 4. commingled 5. regulated together 6. combine 7. congruent

6   COUNTER-, CONTRA-, CONTRO-: against, opposite

Roots
band: ban
mand: order
ven: come (go)
vers: turn

Suffixes
ness: quality of
y: act of

Derivatives   contraband (KON tra band)
contralto (kuhn TRAHL toe)
contrariness (kuhn TRAIR ee ness)
contrary (KON trair ee)
contravene (kan tra VEEN)
controversy (KON trah verse ee)
counter-clockwise (count er KLOK wise)
countermand (count er MAND)

- **against, opposite**   If you move the hands of a clock in a *counterclockwise* fashion, you move them backwards, or _____ their usual direction of movement.

- **It is cancelled.**   If a junior officer's order to her staff is *countermanded* by a senior
  counter: against   officer, what happens to the junior officer's order?
  mand: order   _____

- **opposite, against**   An individual who is *contrary* always seems to get pleasure in taking a(n) _____ view of things. He often irritates others
- **contrariness**   because of this _____.

- **contraband**   Smuggled goods are brought in "against a ban" and thus can be called _____.

- **contralto**   A female whose voice is lower than that of an *alto* is classified as a(n) _____. ("opposite of an alto") A contralto is the lowest woman's voice.

- **against, opposite**   In a *controversy* people are turned _____ each other in attitudes or opinions.

- **go against it**   If a group *contravenes*, does it keep to the law or go against it? _____

SELF-TEST

1. Margaret's _____ made her more interesting to listen to than those with more orthodox opinions. (habit of taking the opposite view)

2. The new environmental protection law was *contravened* by two groups of developers. The law was _____.

3. The court opinion _____ the will of Congress. (canceled; reversed)

4. When the caller gives the signal, the square dancers move in a *counterclockwise* direction. How do they move? _____

5. The Border Patrol seized twenty boxes of watches and other contraband. What is *contraband*? _____

ANSWERS
1. contrariness 2. set aside; ignored; gone against 3. countermanded 4. in reverse; opposite to the direction in which the hands of a clock move 5. goods smuggled or brought in "against the ban"

7 DE-: down, away

Roots | **Suffixes**
celer: quickness, speed | *ate:* verb ending
mot: move | *ation:* act of
pos: put, place
pred: prey, plunder
scend: climb

Derivatives
decelerate (dee CELL er ate)
demote (dee MOTE)
depose (dee POSE)
depredation (dep ruh DAY shun)
depress (dee PRESS)
descend (dee SEND)
detonate (DET uh nate)
devaluate (dee VAL yoo ate)

• **de**

Depress, descend, and *devaluate* all share the prefix _____ meaning "down." Complete the literal meanings of these words:

• **press down**

depress = to _____

• **climb down**

descend = to _____

• **take down or lessen in value**

devaluate = to _____

- **They put him off the throne; remove him from office.**

The people *depose* their king. If *pos* means "put or place," what do they do to him? _____

- **deposed**

Any person who is removed from an office or power can also be said to be _____. ("placed down")

Another meaning of depose is to *take down*, or *record* a statement verbatim for use in a court of law. This statement is called a *deposition*.

- **demote**

To promote a person is to move him forward; to move him down is to _____ him.

- **decelerate**

To accelerate is to speed up (literally, "speed toward"); to slow down is to _____.

- **depredations**

Depredation is an act of making away with plunder, loot, or booty. If a wife wishes to joke about her husband's and children's raids on the cookie jar, she can refer to these raids as _____.

- **detonated**

Occasionally *de* is used merely to intensify the meaning of the root to which it is attached. Thus, *detonate*, which means to set off an explosion, is derived from *ton* (thunder) and means "to make a very thundering sound." We took cover before the dynamite was

_____.

SELF-TEST

1. She ran the car off the road because she realized there was not time to _____. (slow down)

2. The sheepherders were alarmed by the depredations of what they assumed was a wolf pack. What are *depredations*?
_____

3. When Richard Nixon left office, many people felt he was not guilty of any crime, but had been *deposed* for political reasons. *Deposed* means _____.

4. The lawyers grilled him for six hours. He was exhausted by the _____. (act of taking down)

5. The terrorist's bomb _____ prematurely and she was killed. (set off the explosion)

6. The CIA was sufficiently embarrassed by the scandal to *demote* several senior officers. *Demote* means _____.

1. decelerate 2. raids for loot or plunder 3. removed from office; placed down
4. deposition 5. detonated 6. to move down; to move to a lesser position

8   DIS-, DIF-, DI-: apart, not

Roots

comfit: comfort,
   fitting together
consol: comfort,
   cheer
fid: faith
gress: step, go
par: equal
rupt: break
sent: feel

Suffixes

age: verb ending
ate: marked by
ent: marked by
ity: state of
ure: state of

Derivatives

diffident (DIF uh dunt)
digress (deye GRESS)
discomfiture (dis KUM fuh chure)
disconsolate (dis KON suh luht)
disjoint (dis JOINT)
disparage (dis PEAR ij)
disparity (dis PEAR uh tee)
disrupt (dis RUPT)
dissenting (dis SENT ing)

- **disrupt**
  dis: apart
  rupt: break

  To break *(rupt)* apart a class is to _____ it.

- **disjoint**

  To take a chicken apart at the *joints* is to _____ it.

- **disagrees**

  John casts the only *dissenting* vote at a meeting. If *sent* means "feel," John: agrees/disagrees with the group.

- **not**

  The prefix *dis-* can also mean "not." A *disparity* in the ages of two people means they were _____ equal in years. *Disparage* originally meant to marry someone of lower rank. Today it means to belittle someone or something as not equal or not worthy.

- **dis**

  What part of the word *disparage* means *not?* _____

• diffident	The prefix *dif-* is used before a root beginning with an *f*. A person who is shy, who has no self-confidence, is said to be _____. (apart from faith in himself)
• too sad to be cheered up	To console a person is to give her comfort or cheer. If she is *disconsolate*, then she is _____.
• embarrassment, lack of poise	Revealing someone's foolishness or error in front of a group may lead to his discomfiture. *Discomfiture* means _____.
• He gets off onto another topic.	*Gress* means "step." What does a lecturer do when he *digresses* from his stated topic? _____

SELF-TEST

1. Sam was uncharacteristically *diffident* during the interview and failed to make a strong impression. What does *diffident* mean?

2. The speaker _____ so often during her presentation that the audience suspected she was either unprepared or bored with the topic.

3. The defense lawyers made the most of the *disparities* between the testimony of one police officer and another. *Disparities* means _____.

4. Mr. Sims had a nasty habit of _____ both his wife and her cooking. (belittling as not worthy)

5. The Governor felt _____ after losing his bid for re-election. (unable to be consoled)

6. Noticing my discomfiture, the hostess came over and rescued me from Ms. Sanborn. What is *discomfiture?* _____

ANSWERS   1. shy, lacking confidence, "apart from faith" in himself 2. digressed 3. lack of equality, imbalance 4. disparaging 5. disconsolate 6. embarrassment, loss of poise

9   EX-, EF-, E-: out

Other Roots	Suffixes
cis: cut, kill	*acy:* quality of
clud: shut, close	*ate:* verb ending
empt: choose	

fic: do, make, carry on
hale: breathe
ject: throw, hurl
pel: drive
pos: put, place
rad: root

Derivatives   efface (uh FACE)
efficacy (EF fuh kuh see)
eject (ee JEKT)
eradicate (ee RAD uh kate)
excise (eks SIZE)
exclude (eks KLUDE)
exempt (egg ZEMPT)
exhale (eks HALE)

- **out**

Exclude, expel, and *exhale* all share the prefix *ex-*, meaning
_____. Complete the literal meaning of these words.

- **shut out**

exclude = to _____

- **drive out**

expel = to _____

- **breathe out**

exhale = to _____

- **excised**
  ex: out
  cis: cut

A surgeon decides to *cut out* someone's appendix; in his report he will
say he _____ the appendix.

- **do not**

- **ex-**
- **out**

Lawyers are almost always *exempted* from jury duty. Even though you
did not know that *emp* means "choose," you would know that they:
(do/do not) have to serve on juries. The answer comes from the prefix
_____, meaning _____.

- **the ability to carry
  out the desired
  function**
  ef: out
  fic: do, carry on

Fic means "do, make, carry on." To increase the *efficacy* of this medicine, shake it vigorously before using it. *Efficacy* means: the purity of
the product/the ability to carry out the desired function.

- **out**

A headline read, "Exposé of Mafia." Literally *exposé* is "an act of
putting something _____" for public attention.
Usually an *exposé* is an act of showing up some crime or dishonesty.

- **self-effacing**

A person who tries to keep herself from standing out or being noticed (she "faces out or away" from others) is self-_____. In other words, she is extremely modest. *Efface* can have a stronger meaning. To rewrite a passage so that you efface its meaning is to wipe it out or obliterate it.

- **to pull them out by the roots; get rid of them**

If *rad* means "root," what does it mean to *eradicate* weeds? To _____.

- **They were thrown out.**

The drunks were *ejected* from the movie theater. If *ject* means "throw," what was done to them? _____

SELF-TEST

1. Using distilled water increases the efficacy of this product. What does efficacy mean? _____

2. In spite of her outstanding achievements in science, Dr. Edgars has remained a self-effacing woman. *Self-effacing* means _____.

3. Three top officials of the company were named in the newspaper's black-market _____. (act of showing up some crime or dishonesty)

4. Because of his disability, he was _____ from taking physical education. ("chosen out"; freed from)

5. Providing meaningful jobs for more people is the most desirable means of _____ poverty. (getting rid of; pulling out by the roots)

6. A team of surgeons found and _____ a large tumor in her abdomen. (cut out)

ANSWERS

1. the ability of a product to carry out its desired function 2. very modest 3. exposé 4. exempted 5. eradicating 6. excised

10   INTER-: between

Roots	Suffixes
mit: sent	*ent:* marked by
reg: king	*ory:* based on

Derivatives   interject (in ter JEKT)
interlocutory (in ter LOK yuh tore ee)
intermittent (in ter MITT unt)
interracial (in ter RAY shuhl)
interregnum (in ter REGG num)
interstate (IN ter state)

• **between**
An *interstate* trucking firm is a firm that operates
_____ states.

• **interracial**
A marriage between two people of different racial origins is a(n)
_____ marriage.

• **a period of time between kings when no one is on the throne**
If *reg* means "king," what do you think at *interregnum* is?
_____

• **off and on**
Intermittent rains are "sent between" periods of no rain. Thus, *continuous* rain means rain that falls over a long period of time, while *intermittent* rains fall: heavily/off and on.

• **between**
Ject means "throw." If you *interject* a remark into a conversation, you throw it _____ the speech of others. If you cannot get a word in edgewise, you may have to *interject* it!

• **temporary**
John and Mary received an *interlocutory* decree of divorce. If *locut* means "speech or conversation," the decree is made while they are still suing each other for divorce and is therefore: temporary/lasting. Eventually it will be followed by a final decree of divorce.

SELF-TEST

1. His once-famous memory was impaired by intermittent periods of forgetfulness. *Intermittent* means _____.

2. King Henry died and left no heir. The powerful nobles could not agree among themselves on a successor. During the interregnum the country was ruled by Henry's mistress, almost the only person in the court that everyone felt no fear of. What does *interregnum* mean? _____.

3. They were so absorbed in their conversation that she could _____ only a few words. ("throw between")

4. That license has to be approved by the _____ Commerce Commission. ("between states")

5. Adam asked for an interlocutory decree of divorce from Mildred. *Interlocutory* means _____.

6. The new condominium has achieved what its planners hoped it would achieve—not just desegregation but also _____ harmony. ("between races")

1. off and on; occurring from time to time 2. the time between kings 3. interject 4. Interstate 5. temporary decree granted while a divorce case is pending 6. interracial

11   INTRA-, INTRO-: within

Roots	**Suffixes**
mural: walls (of a school)	*al:* relating to
	ion: act of
spect: look	*ly:* adverb ending; manner
ven: vein	
vert: turn	

Derivatives   intramural (in truh MURE uhl)
intrastate (in truh STATE)
intravenous (in truh VEE nuss)
intravenously (in truh VEE nuss lee)
introspection (in truh SPEK shun)
introvert (IN truh vert)
introversion (IN truh ver zhun)

- intramural
- intermural

_____ games are played by teams within the game school. They should not be confused with _____ games, which are between teams from different schools.

- within

- intravenously

An *intravenous* injection is given _____ a vein. Patients who are unable to eat and assimilate food are given nourishment _____. (adverb: in the vein)

- "turns within"
  intro: within
  vert: turn
- introversion

An *introvert* is literally someone who _____. An introvert characteristically is more interested in her own thoughts and feelings than what is going on around her. In general, _____ is the characteristic of preferring to think rather than to act. (act of turning within)

- **"looking within"**
  intro: within
  spec: look

John's imprisonment brought about a long period of *introspection*. Literally, he engaged in the action of _____; he examined his own experience and weighed it thoughtfully.

1. It was surprising that a(n) _____ like Marie would marry an active, outgoing person like Judson. (one who turns within)

2. A faculty team will play against a student team in the first of this year's _____ activities. (within the same school)

3. The introspection forced on him by a long illness made a striking change in his personality. What does *introspection* mean?

   _____

4. In the final stages of her illness Ms. Strang had to be fed *intravenously.* That is, she was fed _____.

1. introvert 2. intramural 3. act of looking within, examining one's own experience
4. by injections in the vein

12   OB-, OC-, OF-, OP-: against

Derivatives
object (ub JEKT, OB jikt)
objective (ub JEKT iv)
obscure (ub SKURE)
obscurity (ub SKURE uh tee)
obstreperous (ub STREP er us)
obstruct (ub STRUKT)
obtuse (ub TOOSE)
occult (uh KULT)
offend (uh FEND)
oppose (uh POSE)

- **"throw against"**
  ob: against
  ject: throw

At our most primitive level of emotions, we might well throw something at a thing or person we did not like. The verb *object* retains some of that idea, since it literally means "to _____." The noun *object* retains some of that idea, too: an *object* is something that can be thrown against. (An *objective* is a target, something you aim at in throwing.)

- **blocks its way**

Obstruct means "build against." A person who tries to *obstruct* justice: helps it along/blocks its way.

- **loud and disorderly; noisy and unruly**

A speaker is plagued by an *obstreperous* group of pickets. If *streper* means "to make a noise," the pickets are being _____.

- **obscured**

To *obscure* something is to put a cover against it and thus to darken it. Mr. Bell's choice of words _____ his meaning. (covered)

- **obscure**
- **not distinct; hard to identify clearly**
- **obscurity**

A poet who is little known (who is in the dark) is a(n) _____ poet. *Obscure* sounds are sounds that are _____. Rachel became famous for writing one good play, then she quickly fell into _____. (darkness; state of being covered against)

- **obtuse**
  ob: against
  tuse: beat

Sometimes a person will appear so dull or stupid that you feel you would like to beat *(tuse)* against him to make him understand. Such a person is _____.

Ob- added to the root *pos* forms the verb *oppose*. You should remember from an earlier discussion of assimilation what happens in a situation like this.

- **op-**
- **oppose**
- **put yourself against that person**

The *ob-* turns into _____ and the word becomes _____. *Pos* means "put"; thus, to oppose someone is to _____.

- **to strike against someone or something**

Fend means "strike." What is the literal meaning of offend? _____

- **occult**

Occult comes from a Latin word *occultus* meaning "hidden" (*Oc-* + *cult* = cover against, cover up). Because it appears to be mysterious and requires knowledge hidden from the average person, astrology is sometimes called a(n) _____ science.

SELF-TEST

1. Ms. Murphy was too *obtuse* to see the point. That is, she was: too busy arguing/hard of hearing/dull and stupid.

2. He claimed to be a member of Sons of Satan, a(n) _____ religious group that believes in and practices black magic. (hidden; requiring knowledge outside the laws of the natural world)

3. Normally Shirley has no trouble in babysitting for the Wodehouses, but last Saturday evening both Hazel and Harry were obstreperous. What does *obstreperous* mean? _____

4. Alice grew up in a(n) _____ part of London called Kentish Town. (not well known; in the dark)

5. The two motorcyclists swore they had done nothing to _____ the law. (build against; hinder)

1. dull and stupid 2. occult 3. noisy, disorderly 4. obscure 5. obstruct

13 PER-: through, thorough, complete

Roots
col: drain
empt: choose
enn: year
forare: bore
meate: pass, go
secut: follow
spic: see
spir: breathe

Suffixes
ate: verb ending
ial: characterized by being
ious: marked by
ity: quality of
ory: marked by

Derivatives

percolate (PER kuh late)
peremptory (per EM ter ee)
perennial (per EN ee uhl)
perforate (PER fer ate)
permeate (PER mee ate)
persecute (PER suh kute)
perspicacious (per spuh KAY shus)
perspicacity (per spuh KASS uh tee)
perspire (per SPIRE)

• **perforate**

What verb means "to bore through" (make a hole in) a piece of paper or cardboard? _____

• **perspire**

Spir means "breathe." When you become very warm, you breathe through the skin, or _____.

- **through the years**
  per: through
  enn: year

Sesame Street is a *perennial* favorite of children. If *enn* means "year," then *perennial* means lasting _____.

- **present everywhere**

Permeate means to pass through. If the odor of cabbage *permeates* a house, it is: present everywhere/apparent only in the kitchen.

- **through**

In the kind of coffeepot known as a *percolator,* boiling water passes _____ ground coffee.

- **punished again and again**

Persecute literally means "to follow thoroughly" (to the end). A person who is *persecuted* is: made famous/punished again and again.

- **sees through things**
  per: through
  spic: see

Uncle Oliver is keen in observing and understanding. He is *perspicacious,* which literally means he _____.

- **perspicacity**

No one else in the family besides Uncle Oliver possesses such _____. (quality of seeing through things)

- **No (she has made an order marked by a thorough or complete choice for you)**
  per: thoroughly
  empt: choose
  ory: marked by

Empt means "choose." Your boss give you a *peremptory* order to work overtime. Does she give you a chance to refuse? _____

SELF-TEST

1. A feeling of patriotism seemed to _____ the crowd. (pass through)

2. I was impressed with the perspicacity of her remarks about social welfare programs. What does *perspicacity* mean? _____

3. The fight ended at once when Father gave us a peremptory order to go upstairs. A *peremptory* order allows no room for _____.

4. A flowering plant that is a *perennial* lives: only one year/from year to year.

5. Spiral notebook paper has a(n) _____ edge so that it can easily be torn out. (bored through; containing holes)

6. After receiving his tenth traffic citation in a week, Hubert shook his head in dismay and said he thought the police were trying to _____ him. (punish again and again)

1. permeate 2. keenness of mind; ability to see through things 3. refusal or further choice 4. from year to year 5. perforated 6. persecute

14   POST-: after

Roots	**Suffixes**
bellum: war	*al:* relating to
lud: movement	*ity:* that which, those who
mort: death	
nat: birth	
part: birth	

Derivatives   postbellum (post BELL uhm)
posterior (poss TEER ee er)
posterity (poss TARE uh tee)
postgraduate (post GRAD yoo uht)
postlude (POST lude)
postmortem (post MORT em)
postnatal (post NATE uhl)
postpone (post PONE)
postwar (POST WAR)

- **after**   *Postwar* problems beset a nation _____ a war.

- **postbellum**   In American history, the South before the Civil War is known as the Antebellum South; the South immediately after the Civil War is known as the _____ South. *Postwar* and *postbellum* mean the same thing, but the latter term is used to distinguish a particular war. If you *postpone* something, you put it _____

- **after**   something else.

- **your "after part," or bottom**   If you sit on your *posterior,* you sit on what? _____

- **after**

If you wish to make the world a better place for *posterity,* you are concerned for your children, those who come _____ you.

- **postnatal**

Prenatal care (before birth) of a baby is equally important as _____ care. (after birth)

- **postgraduate**

For those who desire a higher degree, undergraduate work at a college is followed by _____ work.

- **after death**
  post: after
  mort: death

When the cause of death needs to be ascertained, a postmortem examination is made. *Postmortem* means _____.

- **postlude**

If a *prelude* is a beginning musical piece or movement, a concluding musical piece or movement would be called a(n) _____.

SELF-TEST

1. "Get off your _____; there's work to be done!" growled the sergeant. ("after parts"; bottoms)

2. In her novel Ms. Poindexter gives a realistic description of conditions prevailing in the _____ South. (after the Civil War)

3. We owe it to our posterity to preserve as much of our natural environment as possible. Who are our *posterity?* _____

4. A postmortem examination is required when the cause of death is not known. *Postmortem* means _____.

5. She knew the program was nearly over because the organist had struck up the _____. (concluding musical piece)

6. Darlene had many problems during her pregnancy, but fortunately there were no _____ complications. (after birth)

7. The university had acquired a fine reputation for the quality of its _____ program. (after graduation)

ANSWERS

1. posteriors 2. postbellum 3. those who come after us; our children 4. after death
5. postlude 6. postnatal 7. postgraduate

15   PRE-: before

Roots	Suffixes
mon: warn	*ion:* act of
sent: feel	*ious:* characterized by being
sid: sit	*ment:* result of

Derivatives   precocious (pree KOHSH us)
prefix (PREE fix)
premonition (prem un ISH un)
presentiment (pree ZENT uh munt)
preside (pree ZIDE)
prestressed (PREE STRESSED)
preview (PREE view)

- **prefix**
A word part placed (fixed) before a root is a(n) _____.

- **preview**
A first showing of a play or movie before it is commercially available is a(n) _____.

- **prestressed**
To *prestress* a building material is to introduce internal stress into it so that it will be able to withstand loads applied to it later in a structure of some kind. Today many buildings and other kinds of structures are made of _____ concrete.

- **foreknowledge; an intuitive feeling before the fact is known**
The young mother had a *presentiment* that her child was in trouble. If *sent* means "feeling," what is a *presentiment*? _____

- **presides**
The person in charge of a group usually "sits before" it, controlling the discussion or activities. That is, he _____.

- **a "warning before-hand," often coming in a seemingly mysterious way**
At one time or other you have probably had a *premonition* of danger. If *mon* means "warning," what to you think *premonition* means? _____ *Premonition* is almost identical in meaning to *presentiment,* which you may recall from an earlier section.

- **precocious**
Although *coc* means "cook," the literal meaning of *precocious* is not "precooked" but "cooked ahead of time." In actual usage, a child that develops much ahead of his age is said to be _____.

SELF-TEST

1. The supermarket manager had a(n) _____ that the roof was going to collapse. (feeling or warning before—two different words will fit here)

2. Like so many gifted composers, Mozart was a precocious child. What does *precocious* mean in this context? _____

3. Since the president was ill, she asked the vice-president to _____ at the meeting. (sit before; take charge)

4. The new garage was put up in six days because it was made chiefly of prestressed concrete. *Prestressed* means _____.

ANSWERS

1. premonition or presentiment   2. that he showed musical ability far in advance of his age
3. preside   4. subjected to stress before being built into a structure

16   PRO-: forward, in front of, in favor of

Roots	Suffixes
cliv: lean	*ity:* quality of
create: bring forth	*ion:* act of
fane: shrine, church	
fus: pour	
lix: to be liquid	
pel: push, urge	

Derivatives

proclivity (pro KLIV uh tee)
procreate (PRO kree ate)
profane (pro FANE)
profanity (pro FAN uh tee)
profuse (pro FEWSS)
prolix (PRO lix)
propel (pro PELL)
propose (pruh POSE)

• **forward**

The most common meaning of *pro-* is "forward." To *propel* yourself into politics is to push _____, to go into politics with a great deal of energy.

• tendency	*Cliv* means "lean." To have a *proclivity* for drinking means "act of leaning forward" and thus means: dislike of/tendency.
• propose	The mayor will _____ a new round of budget cuts ("put forward")
• prolix	The mayor is a(n) _____ speaker. (The words keep pouring forward like liquid.) *Prolix* means wordy.
• to reproduce; to bring forth children	The minister believes sex should be solely for *procreation*, not pleasure. What do you think *procreation* means? _____
• you repeat the thanks; "pour forth" thanks	When you give *profuse* thanks to a friend who has done you a favor, what do you do? _____
• worldly	*Pro-* can also mean "in front of." *Profane* language is literally language used "in front of (outside) a shrine or church." In other words, *profane* language is: religious/worldly. This same idea is carried out in the word *profanity*, meaning swearing or the use of crude language.
• pro-British	Occasionally *pro-* means "in favor of," as in *pro-American* or *pro-unionism*. If you take sides on some issue, in favor of the British, you are _____ .

SELF-TEST

1. Roger has a proclivity for getting into trouble with women. What does *proclivity* mean? _____

2. I certainly agree that Senator Phogbound is a prolix speaker. *Prolix* means _____ .

3. If human beings continue to _____ at this rate, the world population will double in 30 years. (bring forth children; reproduce)

4. Ms. Durgess frowned and covered her ears; she was certain Mr. Putnam was going to use _____ language. (crude; full of swearing; not sacred)

5. He made profuse apologies for being so late. Therefore, he apologized: once/over and over.

ANSWERS

1. tendency, inclination, bias 2. wordy; using more words than necessary 3. procreate
4. profane 5. over and over

17   SUB-: under, below

Roots   **Suffixes**
cumb: burden   *anean:* characterized by being
jug: yoke   *ent:* characterized by being
ord: order, control
sid: sit, settle

Derivatives   subarctic (sub ARK tik)
                  subconscious (sub KON shuss)
                  subservient (sub SERVE ee unt)
                  subside (sub SIDE)
                  subjugate (SUB jew gate)
                  subordinate (sub ORD in uht)
                  subterranean (sub ter AIN ee un)
                  succumb (suh KUM)
                  suppress (suh PRESS)

• **under**

A *subordinate* is a person _____ the influence or control of someone else, as in a job or the military. This relationship works best if there is mutual respect. However, if the person who serves under another is slavishly obedient and polite, like a servant, then he is

• **subservient**

_____.

• **under the yoke**
  sub: under
  jug: yoke

Hitler tried to subjugate all of Europe. *Subjugate* translates into "put _____."

• **succumb**

Sub + *cumb* turns into _____ because the *b* in *sub*- assimilates. In the sentence "Denise finally succumbed to the tempta-

• **under**

tion," *succumb* means literally "to fall _____ a bur-den." In the sentence "He *succumbed* to pneumonia," succumb means "died."

• **subside**

When a storm *subsides*, it "settles under" (settles down). It's sad but true: passion is also known to _____.

Write down the derivative that matches the literal meaning:

• **subconscious**

below consciousness = _____

• **subarctic**

below the arctic = _____

• subterranean   below the ground *(terr)* = _____

• suppress   to press under = _____

SELF-TEST
1. Samantha showed her resentment in having to work for Ms. Jones by behaving in a(n) _____ manner. (slavishly obedient or polite)

2. When the excitement of the honeymoon had _____, they discovered they were not very compatible. (settled down)

3. His friends wept when he *succumbed* to AIDS after months of suffering. *Succumb* means _____.

4. Something that is below the surface of the ground is _____.

5. Wild tribespeople living in these mountains have never been subjugated. What does *subjugated* mean? _____.

6. Heading the committee will be John Mercedes and two of his subordinates. What are *subordinates?* _____

ANSWERS
1. subservient 2. subsided 3. to die 4. subterranean 5. brought under the yoke; dominated or tamed 6. people under the influence or control of somebody else

18 SUPER-: over, above, beyond

Roots	Suffixes
flu: flow	*ary:* one who
lat: carry	*ate:* verb ending
numer: number	*ial:* characterized by being
vis: see, look	*ous:* characterized by being

Derivatives   superabundance (soo per uh BUN dunce)
superannuated (soo per ANN yoo ate uhd)
supercharge (SOO per CHARGE)
superficial (soo per FISH uhl)
superfluous (soo PERF loo us)
superlative (soo PERL uh tiv)
supernumerary (soo per NOOM er air ee)
supervisor (SOO per vize er)

- **looks over**
  super: over
  vis: look

A *supervisor* _____ the work of others.

- **superabundance**

After two weeks of workouts, the boxer was *supercharged* with energy. He had a(n) _____ of energy.

- **over**

- **superannuated**

Grandfather Bates's Model T Ford is *superannuated.* Literally that means _____ a year old, but the modern meaning is "out of date, too old for service." People who reach the age of 65 often find they are considered to be _____, too. (outdated) They are forced to retire.

- **superficial**

A *superficial* wound is not serious, since it occurs only on the surface of the body. A shallow remark about a subject, which shows an understanding only at the surface level, can also be called

_____.

- **flowing over**
  super: over
  flu: flow

Any further discussion would be superfluous. *Superfluous* translates into "_____" what is necessary or required.

- **extras**

In the theatre *supernumeraries* are: extras/stars/clowns.

- **superlatives**

Sometimes *super* is better defined as meaning "beyond." If you describe a meal, a performance, or the like in *superlatives,* you use the highest words of praise (you "carry beyond" the usual). Ruth used _____ in describing Grandma Norma's matzoh balls. Typical *superlatives* are adjectives such as "the best," "the finest," "the most fantastic."

SELF-TEST

1. This season Gerald got to see the operas free by working as a(n) _____. (extra)

2. Beware of movies advertised with _____ such as "the most sensational" or "the most expensive" ever made. (excessive words of praise)

3. When the balloon was losing height rapidly, we had to throw overboard everything that was _____. (beyond what was really necessary; overflowing)

4. As younger people take greater shares of corporate responsibility, more middle-aged executives feel *superannuated.* What does *superannuated* mean? _____

5. His sister chided him for making such a superficial remark about religion. What does *superficial* mean? _____

6. If you are *supercharged* with enthusiasm, you have: little/a great deal of enthusiasm.

1. supernumerary 2. superlatives 3. superfluous 4. too old for service; outdated
5. shallow; hitting only the surface 6. a great deal of

19 TRANS-: across, through, beyond

Roots	Suffixes
fer, lat: bear, carry	*ic:* relating to
gress: step, go	*ent:* one who
it: go	*ion:* act of
scend: climb	*ory:* marked by
scrib: write	

Derivatives: transatlantic (trans at LAN tik)
transcend (tran SEND)
transcribe (tran SKRIBE)
transfer (trans FER)
transgression (trans GRESH un)
transient (TRAN shunt)
transitory (TRAN suh tore ee)
translate (trans LATE)
transport (trans PORT)

• **across**

The commonest meaning of *trans-* is "across": a *transatlantic* flight is made _____ the Atlantic Ocean.

• **carried across**
trans: across
port: carry

When goods are *transported*, they are _____ from one place to another.

• **transcribes**
trans: across
scribes: writes

When a secretary "writes across" from a set of symbols to words, we say he _____ his dictation.

- **carries the meaning across from one language to another**

    A person who *translates* languages does what?

    _____

- **transferred**

    Ms. Dobble was _____ from Duluth to St. Paul. ("carried across" from one place to another)

- **transgression**
  trans: across
  gress: step, go

    A person who steps across the line between good and bad commits a moral _____.

- **through**

    Another meaning of *trans-* is "through": A hotel for *transients* is a hotel for people who are passing _____ and not staying long.

- **that it passes by very quickly ("goes through")**

    Poets and philosophers and older people are fond of saying that life itself is *transitory*. What do you think they mean?

    _____

- **beyond**

    Occasionally *trans-* means "beyond." Mr. Edwards transcended his own physical limitations. Here *transcended* means that he "climbed _____" them.

SELF-TEST

1. Reverend Dimmesdale prayed that God would forgive his moral _____. (acts of "stepping across" the line from good to bad)

2. The happiness they shared was _____. (passing quickly; lasting only a brief time)

3. The boarding house displayed a sign that read "Transients Welcome." The manager hoped to rent to what kind of people? _____.

4. In acquiring an education on her own and later becoming a famous writer, she showed that it was possible to transcend the limitations of both poverty and a miserable childhood. *Transcend* means _____.

5. Although it took her a long time, Ms. Forbes was able to _____ Ms. DeVoto's shorthand notes. ("write across")

6. Charles Lindbergh made the first solo _____ flight. (across the Atlantic Ocean)

ANSWERS   1. transgressions 2. transitory 3. passing through, but not staying long 4. climb beyond; get free of 5. transcribe 6. transatlantic

Now that you have studied Latin prefixes, a new look at page 152 might be fun.

6 Less Common Latin Roots

The roots in this chapter are called less important only because fewer words are derived from them. They do account for many useful words, however, and warrant careful study. The following units are structured very simply. Given the literal (and sometimes the current) meaning of the derivatives, you are to match them with the contexts they best seem to fit.

1 ANIM: spirit

Derivatives   animation (an uh MAY shun)—liveliness (state of having much spirit)

magnanimous (mag NAN uh muss)—having a large (generous) spirit

animosity (an uh MAHSS uh tee)—a spirited feeling of ill will or resentment

• animosity   Doreen could not understand Frank's _____ toward her; she had done nothing to offend him.

- **magnanimous**   His donating the land for a new public park was a(n)
                        _____ gesture.

- **animation**   There was not enough _____ in her expression to
                        make her look young and lively in the photograph.

- **animosity**   The Governor barely concealed his _____ toward his
                        opponent after the man attacked his integrity. (ill will)

2   BEL, BELL: war

Derivatives   antebellum (ant ee BELL um)—before the war (especially the
                   Civil War)
                   bellicose (BELL ih kohs)—having a disposition to fight or to
                   start a fight
                   belligerent (buh LIJ er unt)—waging war; actively hostile in
                   mood

Note: Although the meanings of *bellicose* and *belligerent* overlap, *bellicose*
refers more to attitude and *belligerent* more to actual fighting.

- **belligerent**   The Secretary General of the United Nations asked the
                        _____ nations to declare a truce for 36 hours.

- **antebellum**   Many Southern states have attempted to preserve the most impressive
                        of the _____ mansions.

- **bellicose**   Aunt Elizabeth is a bit grumpy at times, but Uncle Henry is by nature
                        nearly always _____. (ready to start a fight)

- **bellicose or belliger-   Norman's _____ statements increased the tension of
  ent (both mean   the men in the prison stockade. (two words will fit here)
  "warlike")**

3   CID, CIS: cut, kill

Derivatives   fratricide (FRAT rih side)—murder of one's brother
                   genocide (JEN uh side)—murder of a race or large group of
                   people
                   incision (in CIZH shun)—act of cutting into; place cut into

infanticide (in FAN tih side)—murder of a very young child
matricide (MAT rih side)—murder of one's mother
patricide (PAT rih side)—murder of one's father

- **fratricide**

Cain slew his brother Abel and thus committed
_____.

- **incision**

Mattie was pleased with her neat _____ and liked to
show it off to friends who came to visit her in the hospital.

- **infanticide**

After the suspicious crib death of her son, she was charged with
_____.

- **matricide**

Electra despised her mother and eventually persuaded her brother to
help her in committing _____.

- **genocide**

After the collapse of Yugoslavia, the Serbs were accused of
_____ in their treatment of the Muslims.

- **patricide**

George was so angry with his father that for a moment he had the urge
to commit _____.

4   COGN: know, be acquainted

Derivatives   cognizant (COG nuh zunt)—knowing; being acquainted with
something
incognito (in cog NEE toe)—disguised; without being known
precognition (pree cog NISH un)—act of knowing ahead of
time

- **incognito**

To avoid being pestered by fans, she traveled _____.

- **cognizant**

He was fully _____ of his duties as a father.

- **cognizant**

At that age I was scarcely _____ of my responsibili-
ties toward my little brothers and sisters.

- **precognition**

Arigo showed psychic ability in several situations, such as the
_____ of his own death.

5 DOC, DOCT: teach

Derivatives   docile (DAHSS uhl)—easily taught
doctrine (DOK trin)—something taught; the body of principles
accepted by believers in a philosophy or school
indoctrinate (in DOK trih nate)—to teach a particular view or
principle
indoctrination (in DOK trih nay shun)—the teaching of a
particular view or principle

• **doctrine**   Some of the younger Puritans gradually began to slip away from the
religious _____ of the elders.

• **indoctrination**   The school's efforts to teach children not to smoke amount to
_____, although in this case it's not a bad thing.

• **docile**   It may be as unfortunate for a child to be too _____
as to be too rebellious.

6 FLEX, FLECT: bend, twist

Derivatives   flexible (FLEKS ih buhl)—able to bend; able to adapt
genuflect (JEN yoo flekt)—bend the knee, as in religious
obedience or in a gesture of respect to royalty
reflection (ree FLEK shun)—act of bending or twisting back;
careful thinking; image

• **reflection**   Narcissus sat beside a clear pool admiring his own
_____ in the water.

• **genuflected**   The priest _____ before leaving the altar.

• **reflecting**   Peter Pan had no memory and therefore lacked the capacity for
_____ on the way he lived.

• **flexible**   My schedule is entirely _____ this afternoon.

7 FRAG, FRACT: break

Derivatives   fractious (FRAK shuss)—unmanageable (breaking out in crossness)
fragile (FRAJ uhl)—delicate (easily broken)
infraction (in FRAK shun)—a violation (a break within)

• **infraction**   He was punished rather severely for a minor _____ of the rules.

• **fragile**   At best, freedom is a(n) _____ possession, easily lost or destroyed. (delicate)

• **fractious**   It was a very _____ young colt—a surprising fact in view of the docile behavior of the mare. (unmanageable)

8 GREG: flock

Derivatives   congregate (KON gruh gate)—flock together; assemble
desegregation (dee seg ruh GAY shun)—abolishment of the practice of segregating blacks and whites, especially in housing and in public schools
gregarious (gruh GARE ee us)—liking to be with others
segregate (SEG ruh gate)—to put into separate groups

• **gregarious**   He was the kind of Irishman we met repeatedly: he was good-natured, witty, and highly _____.

• **segregated**   When immigrants arrived at Ellis Island, some were _____ for supposed mental defects, although many were merely shy or unable to speak English. (put into separate groups)

• **desegregation**   Busing students to different neighborhoods is an unpopular method of school _____.

- **gregarious**   It is not surprising that Martha became a social director on a cruise ship; she has always been a(n) _____ person. (liking to be with others)

- **congregate**   The neighborhood kids used to _____ in the vacant lot beside Charlie's house. (flock together)

9 LUC: light

Derivatives   elucidate (ee LOOSE uh date)—to make clear by explanation (to make light shine out)
lucid (LOO sid)—easy to understand (clear, lighted)
translucent (trans LOO sunt)—allowing light to shine through, but not allowing objects to be distinguished

- **translucent**   The bathroom windows were fitted with _____ glass.

- **elucidate**   The doctor said my medical insurance is inadequate, but he did not _____ the point. (make clear by explanation)

- **translucent**   The greenhouse consisted of an aluminum framework covered with some kind of _____ plastic film. (allowing light to shine through)

- **lucid**   His explanation of the engineering difficulties they encountered was brief but _____. (clear)

10 OMNI: all

Derivatives   omnipotent (ahm NIP uh tunt)—all-powerful
omniscient (ahm NISH unt)—all-knowing
omnivorous (ahm NIV er us)—eating both plant and animal substances (eating all)

- **omnipotent**   One expects a god to be _____, but not a president. (all-powerful)

- **omniscient**   "How should I know what will happen? After all, I am not _____."

• omnipotent

A little boy that age sometimes thinks his father is
_____ and can do almost anything.

• omnivorous

Man is a(n) _____ creature enjoying a wide range of
choices for his dinner table.

SELF-TEST

From the list at the left select the word that best fits each of the following contexts. No word is used twice, and there is one extra word.

• animosity
• belligerent
• elucidate
• fratricide
• genuflect
• gregarious
• incognito
• indoctrinated
• infraction
• magnanimous
• omnipotent

1. The king was safe in the crowd as long as he remained
_____. (disguised)

2. The yard supervisor broke up the fight and ordered the workers to
make peace with each other but both remained
_____. (actively hostile)

3. In his haste to leave, Father Murray almost forgot to
_____ in front of the altar.

4. I felt his _____ reaching out to me from the letter. (ill
will)

5. Ms. Augustine looked at us as though our smiling and laughing were
a(n) _____ of her private code. (violation)

6. Old prospectors like Scotty are not _____, and on
first acquaintance they may even seem antisocial. (liking to be with others)

7. Apart from saying he was going to resign, John did not
_____ his role in the controversy. (explain, clarify)

8. You should ask your father for your allowance now while he is being
so _____. (generous)

9. Several generations of people were _____ in the idea
that might makes right. (taught a belief)

10. The native god did not answer Tawita's prayer, but Tawita was not
dismayed. Native gods were not expected to be either reliable or
_____. (all-powerful)

ANSWERS

1. incognito 2. belligerent 3. genuflect 4. animosity 5. infraction 6. gregarious
7. elucidate 8. magnanimous 9. indoctrinated 10. omnipotent

11   REG, RIG, RECT: rule, straight, right

Derivatives   incorrigible (in KORE ij uh buhl)—unable to be ruled or
controlled
rectify (REK tuh feye)—straighten; make right
rectitude (REK tuh tude)—upright character or conduct;
honesty
regimen (REJ uh mun)—rule; systematic course of therapy or
treatment

• regimen   The dietary _____ prescribed by the doctor limited
him to 600 calories a day.

• rectify   She tried very hard to _____ her mistakes. (make
right)

• incorrigible   I like Barney too, but I must admit that he is a(n)
_____ liar. (uncontrollable)

• incorrigible   Betty will not baby-sit for the Joneses any more; she says their three
children are _____.

• rectitude   The more Reverend Dimmesdale declared his own sin and weakness,
the more he convinced his congregation of his moral
_____. (upright character)

12   SEQU, SECUT: follow

Derivatives   inconsequential (in kon suh KWEN shuhl)—not having
important results following
persecute (PER suh kute)—to torment or punish (to follow
thoroughly)
sequel (SEE kwuhl)—that which follows, as the next
installment of a literary work
sequential (sih KWEN shuhl)—connected in a series (following)

• persecuted   The Mormons were _____ before they migrated to
Utah and founded their own religious colony. (tormented)

- **inconsequential**   The side effects of taking this medicine are _____ when compared with the good it does.

- **sequel**   A rule of thumb is that the _____ of a great film is a pale imitation of the original. (following work)

- **sequential**   The catalogue numbers did not appear to be _____.

- **inconsequential**   The loss of 25 cents and 10 minutes of my time is _____.

13 SON: sound

Derivatives   dissonance (DISS uh nunce)—a combination of sounds that is unpleasant or unharmonious
resonance (REZ uh nunce)—quality of sounding back (echoing)
unison (YOO nuh sun)—sounding as one (one sound)

- **dissonance**   Modern composers no longer avoid _____ in their works, and some even emphasize it. (unharmonious sounds)

- **unison**   The children repeated the poem in _____. (as one)

- **resonance**   There was enough _____ in Mr. Talman's voice that he could be heard without a microphone.

- **resonance**   The box placed below the strings of a violin picks up the sound from the strings and gives it _____.

14 STRING, STRICT: bind tight

Derivatives   astringent (uh STRIN jint)—causing shrinking and contraction (binding tight toward)
constrict (kun STRIKT)—draw together (bind tight with); compress
stringent (STRIN jint)—severe (binding tight)

• **constricted**   Her breathing was _____ by the tight collar.

• **astringent**   After shaving, he used a(n) _____ lotion to firm the skin and erase wrinkles.

• **stringent**   Representatives from student organizations protested the Dean's _____ new regulations. (severe)

• **stringent**   It may require very _____ measures to curb inflation.

15 TANG, TING, TACT, TIG: touch

Derivatives   contingent (kun TIN jont)—depending on something uncertain (touching with)
contiguous (kun TIG yoo us)—in actual contact (touching together)
intact (in TAKT)—whole (not touched)
intangible (in TAN juh buhl)—without a physical basis (not able to be touched)
tangible (TAN juh buhl)—real; having a physical basis (able to be touched)

• **intact**   Few houses were left _____ after the earthquake.

• **tangible**   The judge asked whether there was _____ proof that a crime had been committed. (having a physical basis)

• **contingent**   Our plans for having a picnic tomorrow are _____ on the weather.

• **contiguous**   The two building sites are _____. (in actual contact)

• **contingent**   Building the new house is _____ on being able to sell the old one.

• **intangible**   Success in any field is often based as much on _____ qualities like willpower as on qualifications. (not able to be touched)

16   TEN, TIN, TAIN: hold

Derivatives   incontinence (in KON tih nunce)—lack of self-control (lack of holding together)
tenacious (ten AY shus)—persistent (holding on)
tenure (TEN yer)—possession; length of time of holding or possessing
untenable (un TEN uh buhl)—incapable of being held or defended

• **tenure**   On April 15, Ruby will have 20 years of _____ in this office.

• **incontinence**   We were all offended by the _____ of his language.

• **untenable**   The desertion of his financial supporters left him in a(n) _____ position. (indefensible)

• **untenable**   With her partner's continual complaining and competitiveness, their partnership finally became _____.

• **tenacious**   He was a(n) _____ old man and kept working his claim for weeks after all the other miners had left the mountain.

17   TEND, TENS, TENT: stretch

Derivatives   contentious (kun TEN shus)—quarrelsome (stretching with)
distend (diss TEND)—to stretch apart; overfill
extensive (eks TEN siv)—broad; affecting many things (stretched out)

• **distended**   His stomach was _____ by all the extra food he had eaten.

• **extensive**   The research had covered an extremely _____ field. (wide)

• **contentious**   Lawton did not like working with Belvedere because Belvedere was
_____. (argumentative)

• **contentious**   At the time of their first encounter Ms. Jericho sized up the mayor as
being insecure and _____.

18 TENU: thin

Derivatives   attenuate (uh TEN yoo ate)—weaken; lessen in force (make
thinner)
extenuate (eks TEN yoo ate)—lessen the seriousness of
something by making excuses (thin out)
tenuous (TEN yoo us)—insubstantial (thin)

• **tenuous**   With her standing in the public opinion polls plummeting, the prime
minister had a very _____ hold on power. (thin; insub-
stantial)

• **extenuating**   A criminal often pleads _____ circumstances to jus-
tify his actions. (excusing; lessening seriousness)

• **attenuated**   The agency was reorganized and left with greatly
_____ responsibility for child care and guidance.
(weakened)

• **tenuous**   Ruth's arguments were _____ and unconvincing.
(insubstantial)

19 TRACT: draw, pull

Derivatives   distract (diss TRAKT)—draw away attention (draw apart)
intractable (in TRAKT uh buhl)—stubborn (unable to be pulled
or led)
traction (TRAK shun)—a drawing or pulling

• **intractable**   The baseball owners were _____ in their negotiations, and the players' strike continued. (stubborn)

• **traction**   While the pain persists in the lower back, he will have to remain in
_____. (a drawing or pulling)

• **traction**   The accident occurred because the car could not maintain proper
_____ on the muddy highway.

• **distract**   None of us could _____ the children long enough for
Tamara to hide the Easter eggs.

20   VER: true

Derivatives   veracity (ver ASS suh tee)—truthfulness
verisimilitude (veer uh suh MILL uh tude)—an appearance of
truth or reality (similarity to the truth)
verity (VARE uh tee)—truth; true statement

• **veracity**   Her erratic behavior cast doubt on the _____ of her
testimony. (truthfulness)

• **verisimilitude**   The use of a documentary technique helped to give the movie greater
_____.

• **verities**   Old Man Perkins lectured away at us, confident that he was in touch
with the eternal _____. (truths)

SELF-TEST

From the list at the left select the word that best fits each of the following contexts. No word is used twice, and there is one extra word.

• contentious
• contiguous
• dissonance
• extenuating
• inconsequential
• incontinence
• intractable
• regimen
• stringent
• tangible
• verisimilitude

1. Professor Potter winced at the _____ caused when I
hit the wrong piano keys.

2. Kevin soon regretted the _____ of his language.

3. She needed physical exercise. The _____ prescribed
for her included jogging, swimming, and bicycling.

4. Environmental regulations that are too _____ sometimes get in the way of solving the real problems.

5. The judge admitted there might be _____ factors in
Lady Margery's case, but he couldn't reduce her sentence.

6. Director Oliver Stone took liberties with the events surrounding the Kennedy assassination in the movie "*JFK*," but many viewers were taken by the film's _____.

7. The four of us pleaded with him to change his mind, but Matthew remained _____. (stubborn)

8. Washington and Oregon are _____ states. (their borders touch)

9. The atmosphere in Congress was so _____ that there was legislative gridlock. (quarrelsome)

10. The manager dismissed the matter of repairs, saying it was _____.

1. dissonance 2. incontinence 3. regimen 4. stringent 5. extenuating 6. verisimilitude 7. intractable 8. contiguous 9. contentious 10. inconsequential

Now that you've mastered this chapter, you might enjoy a new look at the drawing that opens it on page 186.

SEPTIFEATHERED

HEPTAFEATHERED

7 Greek and Latin Numerals

English	Greek	Latin
one	mono	uni
two	di	du
three	tri	tri
four	tetra	quadr
five	penta	quint
six	hexa	sex
seven	hepta	sept
eight	oct	oct
nine	ennea	nov
ten	dec	dec
hundred	hecto	cent
thousand	kilo	mill

Very few English words are derived from the Greek root *ennea,* and even these are infrequently used: *Ennead, enneagon.* Similarly, only a few common words are derived from the Latin root *nov: November* (the ninth month in the old Roman calendar), *novena* (in the Roman Catholic church, saying prayers or holding services on nine days).

In the metric system, the Greek root *deca* is used to mean ten: *decade* (ten years). The Latin root *deci* is used to mean one tenth ($\frac{1}{10}$): *decimal*, *decimate* (kill one in ten). The Greek root *hecto* means one hundred: *hectoliter* (100 liters); the Latin root *centi* also means one hundred but is commonly used to mean one hundredth ($\frac{1}{100}$): *centiliter* (one hundredth of a liter). The Greek root *kilo* means one thousand: *kilometer* (one thousand meters); the Latin root *milli* means one thousandth ($\frac{1}{1000}$): *millimeter* (one thousandth of a meter).

SELF-TEST

1. If you speak in one tone of voice, you speak in a: bitone/monotone.

2. How many babies are born at the same time if there are *quintuplets*? _____

3. A figure or area with four angles is a: quadrangle/triangle.

4. A famous five-sided building near Washington, D.C., is called the: Pentagon/Octagon.

5. An athlete who can compete in ten different sports events enters what contest in the Olympic games? (the hexapod/the decathlon)

6. How many instrumentalists are featured in an *octet?* _____

7. A state with a *unicameral* legislative system has: two legislative bodies/one legislative body.

8. A person in his seventies is called a: sexagenarian/septuagenarian.

9. In the metric system one hundred grams would make up a unit called a: hectogram/milligram.

10. A *milliliter* of water would be: one thousand liters/one thousandth of a liter.

11. The Ten Commandments can also be called the: Eulogy/Decalog.

12. Richard estimates we will have to drive another fifteen _____ to reach Paris. (use the Greek root for thousand)

13. If you speak four languages, you are _____. (use the Latin root)

14. The specimen was *trisected.* It was cut into how many parts? _____

15. This creature is the only one of its kind. It is therefore _____. (use the Latin root)

16. A worm-like creature that seems to have a hundred feet is a(n)
    _____. (use the Latin root for hundred)

17. The New Year 2000 is known as the third _____.
    (use the Latin root)

18. An athlete who wishes to compete in only five different sports events
    enters what contest in the Olympic games? (the pentathlon/the
    enneathlon)

19. A *century* is a period of how many years? _____

20. A fair celebrating the one hundredth birthday of something is a: (cen-
    tennial/perennial) affair.

ANSWERS   1. monotone 2. five 3. quadrangle 4. Pentagon 5. decathlon 6. eight 7. one legislative
body 8. septuagenarian 9. hectogram 10. one thousandth of a liter 11. Decalog
12. kilometers 13. quadrilingual 14. three 15. unique 16. centipede 17. millennium
18. the pentathlon 19. one hundred years 20. centennial

If you missed it the first time around, your new knowledge of Greek
and Latin numerals should now unlock the fowl mystery on page 202.

8 Confusables

As this book has shown, many English words are formed from standard parts—roots modified by a number of prefixes and suffixes—to produce precise meanings. In this, the language is not very different from any number of manufactured items like cars. Modern cars are so similar that people tend to mix them up. You can always tell a Ferrari from a Rolls Royce, but it's much harder to distinguish a Toyota from a Nissan or Buick, particularly in traffic. Thus, words that are very much alike, such as *accept* and *except,* may be confused.

Some words that sound alike, but have nothing to do with one another, can also be confused, such as *appraise* and *apprise.* Others are confused because they are part of a set, even if they are antonyms. *Infer* and *imply* are an example. The words are very similar and in the heat of conversation or writing to a deadline, the mind may jump the rails and substitute one for another. Or, very likely, the speaker or writer never learned the difference. In other cases, the confusion is between words and *nonwords*—corruptions of real words that are so common that people don't know what the real word is at all. *Regardless* and *irregardless* are the best example. The first is a word, and the second isn't.

But plenty of people *do* know the correct usage, and in their eyes and ears, when you use the wrong word you may look ignorant, or be seriously misunderstood.

Sometimes even people who do know the difference will make embarrassing mistakes. The spell-check function on computers and word processors presents a new dimension to this problem. Some of the examples in this chapter were seen in the *New York Times* and were surely written by people who do known the correct word. Fast typists and writers or journalists on deadline will type the word *passed* when they mean *past*, or *lead* when they mean *led*. A spell checker will not catch these mistakes.

The following list is by no means complete. I've chosen the confusables that I find carry the most serious possibility of misunderstanding day to day and that I find most irritating.

accept—except   The confusion in spoken language doesn't make a difference because these words sound identical. But look out in your writing. They're almost antonyms. *Accept* means to take in or receive. As a verb, *except* means to exclude. As a preposition *except* means unless.

adverse—averse   Both are adjectives that mean *against*, but they can't be used interchangeably.

Abstractions are *adverse*: Everything the president did provoked *adverse* public reactions.

People are *averse*, if they are mildly against something: I am *averse to* buying merchandise from strangers who call me in the middle of dinner.

advice—advise   *Advice* is a noun, something you give to people who are in need of guidance. *Advise* is a verb. You *advise* people who need *advice*.

affect—effect   *Affect* is almost always a verb, and *effect* is almost always a noun. People often mix them up.

For example: Tickling has no *affect* on me. This is wrong. Use *effect*.

Voting for one party or another doesn't *effect* the direction of government policy. Wrong again. Use *affect*.

all ready—already   The first is an adjective that merely implies that everything is ready. The second is an adverb that refers to a particular time: The children were *all ready* to play, but their parents were *already* exhausted.

all right—alright   If *already* is a word, why not *alright*? Because it's not. Words change all the time to reflect the way people use them even if they're not correct by the standards your English teachers grew up with. But some haven't been accepted yet, and this is one of them.

all together—altogether   *All together* means that several or many are being treated as one. *Altogether* means *totally* or *as a whole*. The members of the choir seldom sang *all together.* I was *altogether* disgusted with the way she treated her mother.

allude—elude   *Allude* means to refer to something indirectly. For example: I didn't want to call John an embezzler, so I *alluded* to my feelings by saying that his books didn't balance.

elude means to *escape.* For example: He *eluded* prosecution by going to Switzerland.

all ways—always   *All ways* means in every respect, or every method of doing things. I seemed to be going *all ways* at once. *Always* means at all times. "I will love you *always.*"

alternate—alternative   You hear the word *alternate* used frequently in the phrase *alternate jurors.* This is probably an old legal term, but it really should be *alternative jurors. Alternate* as an adjective means taking place by turns. For example: My wife and I make dinner on *alternate* days.

Alternative means a choice is available. For example: A college basketball player who finishes his degree may have an *alternative* career if he does not succeed in professional basketball.

alternately—alternatively   Adverbs that follow the same thinking expressed previously.

ambiguous—ambivalent   *Ambiguous* suggests lack of clarity and the existence of possible alternative meanings in writing, evidence, or words. For example: She told me she loved me, but because she couldn't look me in the eye when she said it, her message was *ambiguous.*

Ambivalent refers to conflicting feelings. For example: I felt *ambivalent* about marrying her because I wasn't sure she loved me.

apprise—appraise   These two words are confused because they sound similar but they have nothing in common.

Apprise means to inform. For example: The police failed to *apprise* him of his rights when they arrested him, so the judge set him free.

Appraise means to estimate the value of something. For example: The jeweler will *appraise* your mother's ring and *apprise* you of its value.

avoidance—evasion   *Avoidance* is keeping your distance from something. *Evasion* is resorting to tricks or dishonesty to accomplish the same thing. This is one that any accountant can help you with. Tax *avoidance* is acceptable because you use legal means to keep from paying more taxes. Tax *evasion* is against the law.

beside—besides   *Beside* means next to, compared with, or irrelevant. *Besides* means in addition to. When I walked into the room, there was no one sitting *beside* him. The sergeant asked for volunteers, but no one stepped forward *besides* me.

blatant—flagrant *Blatant* is bad and obvious. The insurance agent accused them of *blatant* lying in their account of the accident and refused to pay their claim. *Flagrant* is bad and scandalous. One of the most common uses of *flagrant* is in sports. If an offense on the basketball court is bad enough, it is said to be a *flagrant* foul and warrants an extra penalty.

canvas—canvass *Canvas* is the cloth that sails are made of. *Canvass* means the questioning of large numbers of people about how they intend to vote, about their behavior, attitudes, or what they might have seen when a crime was committed nearby.

caramelized—carmelized There is no such word as *carmelized*. When you cook sugar to a syrupy brownish state, you are caramelizing it.

censor—censure *Censor* means to suppress words, ideas, photographs, or other material deemed unacceptable. *Censure* means to reprimand. The Senator's accusations are irresponsible, but can't be *censored*. His colleagues will *censure* him for his actions.

childlike—childish *Childlike* means innocent. That's good. *Childish* means immature. That's bad.

cohesive—coherent The Latin root of both words—*cohere*—means stick together. The distinction lies in what is doing the sticking. People or objects that stick together are *cohesive*. Ideas, arguments, and trains of thought that make sense are *coherent*.

collaborate—corroborate *Collaborate* means work together: Gilbert and Sullivan *collaborated* on many operettas. *Corroborate* means to provide additional evidence: I couldn't find another witness to *corroborate* my testimony.

compare—contrast To *compare* is to study both differences and similarities. To *contrast* is to concentrate only on differences.

complacent—complaisant *Complacent* means self-satisfied. *Complaisant* means willing to please.

complement—compliment A *complement* makes something complete: Ira Gershwin's lyrics were the ideal *complement* for his brother's music, and together they wrote perfect songs. A *compliment* is an expression of praise: The only honest *compliment* I could pay him was to say that his impractical ideas were highly imaginative.

complement—supplement Unlike a *complement,* a *supplement* is added to a quantity that's already complete: I took a part-time job to *supplement* my pension.

concave—convex The inside surface of a contact lens is *concave*. The outer surface is *convex*.

connote—denote *Connote* suggests qualities in addition to its dictionary meaning. *Denote* is the basic dictionary meaning itself. For example: It's morning in America. Morning *denotes* a time of day. But it also *connotes* a time of light after darkness, of optimism after despair.

contemptible—contemptuous *Contemptible* means *deserving* contempt; *contemptuous* means *showing* contempt.

continual—continuous—continuing—constant *Continual* means proceeding with some let up. *Continuous* means proceeding without let up. *Continuing* means proceeding without end. *Constant* means proceeding without change.

criterion—criteria *Criteria* is the plural of *criterion*.

cynic—skeptic A *cynic* always looks for the worst in people, events, and motives. A *skeptic* occasionally looks on the bright side, but is alert to the possibility that things are really worse than they look.

decimate—defeat—destroy The Latin prefix *deci-* means a tenth, and *decimate* meant to kill a tenth of a group. That's a pretty bad defeat. But now most people use *decimate* when they really mean *destroy* or *obliterate*, both of which suggest total destruction.

detract—distract *Detract* means to take away from or diminish. For example: Knowing that the Congressman was cruel to his wife *detracts* from our ability to take his family-values program seriously.

Distract means to divert attention. For example: A craving for chocolate *distracted* me from my work.

diagnosis—prognosis A *diagnosis* tells a sick person what's wrong with her. A *prognosis* tells the person whether and when she's likely to get better.

disburse—disperse *Disburse* means to pay out money. *Disperse* means to scatter.

discriminating—discriminatory *Discriminating* means having high standards of judgment and taste. *Discriminatory* means biased or prejudiced.

disinterested—uninterested *Disinterested* means objective. Many people use this word when they really mean uninterested. A referee should be *disinterested*. My son is frequently *uninterested* in his homework.

emigrant—immigrant—émigré An *emigrant* has left his or her country. An *immigrant* has settled in another country. An *émigré* is someone who has left his or her own country for reasons of principle or politics.

eminent—imminent—immanent *Eminent* means well-known and respected. *Imminent* means coming soon. *Immanent* means present in.

emotive—emotional *Emotive* means provoking strong emotions: The photographs of the crime scene were so emotive that members of the victim's family turned away. *Emotional* means feeling or displaying strong emotions: The defendant showed no *emotional* reaction to the long sentence.

empathy—sympathy *Empathy* means the capacity to experience the feelings of another person. For example: My *empathy* with his misery was so strong that I wept along with him.

Sympathy means an identification with someone else's plight, but more intellectually and less emotionally than suggested by *empathy*. For example: My *sympathy* with her plight made me want to help her.

enervate—energize These are antonyms. *Enervate* means to sap energy. *Energize* means to supply energy.

envelop—envelope *Envelop,* a verb, means to wrap or enclose. *Envelope* is a container for a letter.

ecology—environment *Ecology* is the science of living things and how they relate to their environment. It is not the *environment* itself. Thus, we never damage an *ecology,* but we regularly damage our *environment.*

facetious—sarcastic *Facetious* means joking. *Sarcastic* means mocking.

fallacious—fallible *Fallacious* means containing a flaw or fallacy. *Fallible* means capable of making a mistake.

few—less *Few* refers to numbers of individuals. *Less* refers to volumes. For example: I drink *fewer* beers than I used to. In other words, I drink *less* beer.

The confusion may arise from the fact that the opposite of both words is *more.*

flammable—inflammable Keep both *flammable* and *inflammable* materials away from open flames. They both indicate that the materials can easily be set afire. The opposite is *nonflammable.*

flaunt—flout *Flaunt* means to display proudly or ostentatiously. For example: The crime king *flaunted* his wealth with expensive cars, jewelry, and houses.

Flout means to disobey openly or scornfully. For example: The crime king owned expensive cars, jewelry, and houses because he *flouted* the laws against gambling, prostitution, and narcotics.

flounder—founder To *flounder* is to exert great effort and get nowhere. For example: He got caught in the riptide and *floundered.* No matter how hard he swam, he moved no closer to shore. Or: She *floundered* in trigonometry until the teacher gave her individual help.

To *founder* is to hit an obstacle and sink, collapse, or fail: The ferry hit a rock in the channel and *foundered*. The passengers had to be picked up by rescue boats.

forbear—forebear *Forbear* means to show patience. *Forebear* is an ancestor.

forego—forgo *Forego* means precede. A form of this words appears most frequently in the term *foregone conclusion,* which is a conclusion reached in advance.

Forgo means *give up.*

fortuitous—fortunate *Fortuitous* describes an event that occurs by chance. *Fortunate* means that whatever happened was good for the individuals involved. For example: Our meeting in town was *fortuitous.* I was *fortunate* that he had the money he owed me in his wallet.

genteel—gentle *Genteel* connotes good manners and good breeding. *Gentle* means mild.

good—well *Good* is an adjective. *Well* is usually an adverb, but is also an adjective. The most common mistake occurs in the following exchange: How are you? I'm *good.*

This person probably is asking about the other person's health, so the proper answer would be "I'm *well.*"

hanged—hung A murderer may be *hanged.* News of his execution would be *hung* on a public notice board to let the people know. In other words, people are *hanged* and things are *hung.*

home—hone The phrase *home in* has recently contracted a case of mistaken identity. It is now frequently pronounced *hone in.* This is wrong. *Home in* means to get closer and closer to a goal, destination, or solution. Think of a *homing* pigeon. There's no such thing as a *honing* pigeon. *Hone* means to sharpen, as in *honing a knife* or *honing an argument.*

honorary—honorable *Honorary* means awarded in a ceremonial way, without being earned. *Honorable* means worthy of honor. For example: This year's *honorary* degree goes to the *Honorable* Judge Hugo Hackenbush.

I—me *I* is the subject. *Me* is the object. Plenty of people who really ought to know better say things like "Between you and I." It should be "you and me."

imply—infer *Imply* is what a speaker or writer does with words. *Infer* is what a listener or reader does with them: "Are you *implying* that I'm paranoid?" "No, but with your suspicious mind, you are *inferring* that I think so."

invaluable—valueless *Invaluable* means even more valuable than valuable. It's so valuable that you cannot place a value on it. *Valueless* means completely lacking in value.

inveigh—inveigle *Inveigh* (against) means to denounce quite adamantly, maybe violently. *Inveigle* is to get your way through cleverness or underhanded means.

irrespective—irregardless *Irrespective* is a real word meaning without regard. For example: He went on with his work *irrespective* of our objections.

There is *no such word* as *irregardless*.

its—it's *Its* is the possessive of it. *It's* is a contraction of *it is*.

libel—slander If you say something about me that isn't true and damages my reputation, I sue you for *slander*. If a newspaper publishes the falsehood, I sue it for *libel*.

media—medium Television, newspapers, and radio are all *media*. However, one of them at a time is a *medium*.

migrate—emigrate In a mobile society, it's important to understand the difference. When you move from New York to California, you are *migrating*. When you move to Mexico, you're *emigrating*.

mitigate—militate *Mitigate* means to lessen bad effects. *Militate* means to have strong influence. The phrase *militate against* is frequently said incorrectly as *mitigate against*.

obsolete—obsolescent *Obsolete* means out of date or no longer in use. *Obsolescent* means not obsolete yet but getting there.

oculist—optician—optometrist—ophthalmologist An *oculist* is a doctor who specializes in eye problems. An *optician* makes and sells eyeglasses. An *optometrist* tests the refraction and range of the eye and figures out how strong your glasses should be. An *ophthalmologist* is a scientist (often a physician) who studies the eye and its diseases.

official—officious *Official* means possessing formal authority. For example: Only the public relations department is permitted to make *official* announcements on behalf of senior management.

Officious means asserting petty authority. For example: The *officious* clerk at the motor vehicles department branch made me wait in line for 20 minutes when he could have told me that I could renew my license by phone.

ordinance—ordnance An *ordinance* is a law or rule. *Ordnance* is military supplies, especially artillery shells.

overlook—oversee *Overlook* usually means fail to see, disregard, or excuse. It can also mean observe from high ground. *Oversee* means supervise.

passed—past *Passed* is either the past tense or past participle of the verb *to pass*. *Past* can be a noun, adjective, adverb, or preposition. For example:

(noun) He had a checkered *past*.

(adjective) She took pride in *past* achievements.

(adverb) She honked the horn as she drove *past*.

(preposition) He whistled as he walked *past* the cemetery.

pedal—peddle As a noun, *pedal* is the thing you push with your foot while riding a bicycle or driving a car. As a verb, *pedal* means push the *pedal* on the bicycle. *Peddle* means sell.

perquisite—prerequisite *Perquisite* generally means a special benefit or privilege in addition to salary, such as eating in the executive dining room or an employee discount. These are colloquially called *perks*.

A *prerequisite* is something required ahead of time. For example: chemistry and biology are *prerequisites* for medical studies.

persecute—prosecute *Persecute* means single out for abuse. *Prosecute* means bring legal action against. A person who is being *prosecuted* without substantial evidence may claim that she is being *persecuted*.

personal—personnel *Personal* refers to matters affecting or relating to an individual person. *Personnel* refers to people within an organization.

perverse—perverted *Perverse* means stubborn, deliberately contrary, or wrongheaded. *Perverted* means deviant.

phenomenon—phenomena *Phenomenon* is the singular form of *phenomena*.

precipitate—precipitous *Precipitate* means rash, or too hasty. For example: His *precipitate* decision cost the company millions of dollars in legal fees.

Precipitous means steep and can be used to convey difficulty. For example: *Precipitous* business conditions made it unlikely that the company would survive.

principal—principle This one has been drummed into the heads of everyone who ever sat in an English class. Yet the two words are regularly mistaken for one another, especially when the writer is in a hurry. *Principal*, either as a noun or as an adjective, means *chief*. For example:

My *principal* concern is for the welfare of my family. (adjective)

The school *principal* was a stern disciplinarian. (noun)

My investment objective was to protect the *principal*, rather than take big risks for a higher rate of interest. (noun)

Principle is a noun, and it refers to a basic truth in fields like law, ethics, and science. For example: I would never violate a *principle* no matter how much money you paid me.

prodigy—protégé   A *prodigy* is a young person with a distinct talent who achieves at levels well beyond the level associated with his or her age. A *protégé* is someone who is being helped by a patron or mentor.

psychiatrist—psychologist   Although there may be some overlap in the kinds of treatment they provide, a *psychiatrist* is a medical doctor, licensed to prescribe medication. A psychologist has nonmedical qualifications and generally doesn't treat mental diseases.

rebound—redound   *Rebound* means to bounce back. For example: A basketball *rebounds* from the backboard. She *rebounded* from her illness and threw herself into her work.

Redound means to have an effect. For example: Despite the pain and suffering it caused, the accident *redounded* to my great financial gain after the lawsuit was settled.

reek—wreak   *Reek* means *smell terrible*. *Wreak* means *cause*, almost invariable with a bad effect. For example: computer games *wreak* havoc with my work habits.

re-count—recount   *Re-count* means count again. *Recount* means to narrate or tell a story. For example: I loved listening to my father and uncles *recount* tales of life in the old neighborhood.

Note: there are other words beginning with *re* that involve the same kind of distinction.

sew—sow   *Sew* is what you do with a needle and thread. *Sow* means to plant seeds, suspicion, and other things that grow from very small to much larger.

shrank—shrunk   *Shrank* is the past tense of *shrink*. *Shrunk* is the past participle. *Shrunk* was often used instead of shrank before the movie "Honey, I Shrunk the Kids" came out, but even the movie didn't make it acceptable for correct English.

The correct usage: My socks *shrank* in the wash. Either my pants *had shrunk* in the wash, or I had gained five pounds.

sprang—sprung   Same distinction as *shrank* and *shrunk*. Both are forms of the verb *spring*. For example: When he swore at me, I *sprang* at his throat. The argument *had sprung* from a misunderstanding about the cost of the new dress.

shear—sheer   *Shear* is a verb meaning to cut closely. For example: He *shears* sheep for a living.

Sheer is an adjective that means pure (as in *sheer luck*), vertical (as in *sheer cliff*), or thin and nearly transparent (as in *sheer fabric*).

silicon—silicone The distinction between these words is very important in the new economy of the United States. *Silicon* is a substance found in sand and used in computer chips. Hence the name Silicon Valley, which refers to the part of California where much of the U. S. computer industry is based. *Silicone* means organic compounds of silicon. It is used in paints, varnishes, and lubricants. Most prominently, it has been used in breast implants.

simple—simplified—simplistic *Simple* means *easy* or *uncomplicated,* which is generally a good thing. For example: His *simple* explanation of the theory of relativity made it comprehensible to us for the first time.

    Simplified is a verb that means *made simpler:* She could cook better than I could, so she *simplified* her recipes for us, and the result as almost as good as hers, but not quite.

    Simplistic means reduced to an *excessively simple* extent, which is not so good. For example: His plan to force teenage mothers to find jobs was *simplistic* because it made no provision for what the mothers should do with their children while they were at work.

spare—sparse Both mean *meager,* but they are used in different ways: Bodies are *spare* if they are lean, without much fat. So is writing. It tells the story efficiently without too many descriptions, asides, or adjectives. Populations, crops, and hair are *sparse,* if people, plants, or hair are thinly scattered over an area.

specious—spurious *Specious* means apparently true, but unable to bear up under close examination. *Spurious* means untrue, false, or based on wrong ideas.

stationary—stationery *Stationary* means not moving. *Stationery* is the noun for writing materials.

strait—straight *Strait* means a narrow strip of water between two large bodies of land, such as the Bering Strait between Asia and Alaska, or a state of confusion or difficulty, as in *dire straits.* Both have to do with *tightness.* It has nothing to do with the shortest distance between two points, as in *straight* line. Never make the mistake of referring to a *straight jacket.* Think of a *tight jacket.* Or if you feel that your financial situation is getting tighter all the time, say you are in *straitened* circumstances. However, if you hair is too curly, by all means have it *straightened.*

strategy—stratagem—tactics *Strategy* means the planning for some large, long-term campaign—usually military or business. For example: He hoped that his *strategy* would allow his company move into second place in the competitive home-computer market in three years' time.

Stratagem is a ploy or trick aimed at deceiving someone else. For example: Our researcher often pretended to be a business student when she called our competitors, a *stratagem* that allowed her to get information about them more simply than she would have by telling the truth.

Tactics are the art and science of accomplishing a goal, such as deployment of troops or resources in a military battle. For example: Rather than send in ground troops right away, his *tactics* called for two days of round-the-clock bombing, followed by dropping leaflets inviting the enemy to defect.

till—until—'til   *Till* and *until* mean the same thing. Many people think that *till* is incorrect, and that it should be written *'til*. They are wrong.

tortuous—torturous   *Tortuous* means having many twists and turns. For example: She took a *tortuous* route along back roads instead of driving directly on the freeway. His explanation about his whereabouts at the time of the robbery was so *tortuous* that we didn't believe his alibi, and he became the primary suspect.

Torturous pertains to torture or pain—physical or mental. For example: They finally got tired of the mutual deceptions and insults, and ended their *torturous* marriage.

vice—vise   A *vice* is a bad habit or anti-social practice, like gambling, drinking, or using drugs. A *vise* is a device used in a workshop to hold wood or other materials in place; it is correctly pronounced the same as *vice* and wrongly written that way.

who's—whose   *Who's* is short for *who is* or *who has*. For example: I know *who's* responsible for this anonymous accusation, and I will punish him.

Whose is the possessive form of *whom*. For example: *Whose* woods these are I think I know.

worthless—priceless   *Worthless* means *without worth* or *without value*. *Priceless* means the opposite—that something is so valuable that a price can't be placed on it.

yoke—yolk   *Yolk* is the yellow part of an egg. A *yoke* is a wooden harness used to keep oxen side by side. It can be used when referring to any close relationship. For example: They were yoked in common purpose and worked 'round the clock to finish their report.

SELF-TEST   The following are a number of sentences and paragraphs written to test your grasp of the distinctions between many of the confusables discussed earlier. Each numbered, italicized word is one of the confusables, correct or incorrect. At the end of each passage, write "correct" or, if you believe the word is incorrect, write the correct word in the space next to it. The answers are listed at the end of the section. Read the entire sentence to understand the context of the word.

1. The jurors gasped as the (a) *emotive* photographs were shown in the courtroom, but the supporting evidence failed to (b) *collaborate* the testimony of the eyewitness.

   a. _____
   b. _____

2. The presiding judge, the (a) *Honorary* Hugo Hackenbush, thought the evidence was (b) *ambiguous* and the testimony complicated. While the (c) *persecutor* gave a (d) *cohesive* explanation of the (e) *tortuous* events, the defense had evoked plenty of (f) *sympathy* for the defendant, which could create reasonable doubt, or the defense could argue in its closing that there were (g) *militating* circumstances.

   a. _____
   b. _____
   c. _____
   d. _____
   e. _____
   f. _____
   g. _____

3. The rock star returned to his hometown and (a) *flaunted* his new wealth. One of his former neighbors grumbled, "I knew him when he (b) *sheered* sheep for spending money." Another said, "I'd like to put his head in a (c) *vice* and give his ego a squeeze." A third remarked, "He's so (d) *contemptible* of our way of life."

   a. _____
   b. _____
   c. _____
   d. _____

4. Still, the townspeople were (a) *enervated* by the visit of their most (b) *imminent* former resident, and they turned out by the hundreds to spruce the town up in advance of his arrival. A (c) *canvass* of the town by the (d) *media* found that most of the townspeople were very proud. Thus it came as a great surprise when the government indicted him for income tax (e) *avoidance.*

   a. _____
   b. _____
   c. _____
   d. _____
   e. _____

5. "(a) *Irregardless* of the improvement in my condition," she said, "I still don't feel (b) *good* enough to go back to work. Anyone (c) *whose* accusing me of malingering is guilty of (d) *slander.*"

   a. _____
   b. _____
   c. _____
   d. _____

6. Her doctor agreed. "The medication is having no (a) *effect,*" he said. "And the search for the right treatment continues to (b) *allude* us. Between you and (c) *me,* I think we're (d) *overseeing* something crucial, and we will need to perform more tests." In the meantime, the doctor sent her to a (e) *psychologist* to prescribe her some anti-depressants.

   a. _____
   b. _____
   c. _____
   d. _____
   e. _____

7. "Our air strikes dropped so much (a) *ordinance* on the enemy positions that we completely (b) *decimated* their army," the general told the press (c) *corpse* in the early weeks of the war. In time, however, his (d) *spurious* account of the battle (e) *redounded* to his detriment. Not only had many of the enemy survived, but (f) *less* of the enemy's crack troops were killed than had been announced. Most of the bodies on the (g) *corps*-strewn battlefield turned out to be civilians.

   a. _____
   b. _____
   c. _____
   d. _____
   e. _____
   f. _____
   g. _____

8. "Don't expect a lot of (a) *prerequisites* on this job, like expense accounts and company cars," said the recruiter. "Love of hard work is the most important (b) *perquisite,* and honesty is the most important (c) *principal.*" After several months on the job, however, I recognized just how (d) *simplified* this speech had been. There were many executives whose actions seem motivated solely by the quest for free meals and frequent flier miles. Their contribution to the company was (e) *priceless.*

   a. _____
   b. _____

c. _____

d. _____

e. _____

9. The civil engineer said, "The most important (a) *criteria* for the new highway is that rain shouldn't collect on the driving surface. Therefore, it must be (b) *convex* rather than flat."

    a. _____

    b. _____

10. "Our (a) *diagnosis* is that her problems are caused by inhaling large amounts of (b) *silicon* lubricants at the machine shop," said the doctor.

    a. _____

    b. _____

11. The judge found that the fast-food chain was (a) *discriminating* in its promotion practices, and ordered that an affirmative-action program be put in place.

    a. _____

12. The (a) *official* receptionist took great delight in making people wait as long as he could for their appointments. When he was asked questions, there were no (b) *simplified* answers. He never felt satisfied unless people remained in the waiting room 30 minutes (c) *past* their appointment times.

    a. _____

    b. _____

    c. _____

13. The advance of computer technology is so rapid that each generation of (a) *silicone* chips is (b) *obsolescent* almost as soon as it's introduced. A comprehensive corporate (c) *stratagem* should take this into account.

    a. _____

    b. _____

    c. _____

14. I was (a) *detracted* by the floaters in the corner of my field of vision, so I went to an (b) *optician* to see if there was anything organically wrong with my eyes.

    a. _____

    b. _____

15. Behind her (a) *childlike* demeanor was a (b) *discriminating* mind and a (c) *cynical* sense of humor. She could cut people to the quick with her (d) *facetious* comments.

    a. _____
    b. _____
    c. _____
    d. _____

16. The doting grandparents went out of their way to ensure that the pajamas they bought for the new baby were (a) *inflammable.* Safety was a (b) *perquisite* for any gift they bought for their grandchildren.

    a. _____
    b. _____

17. She (a) *all ways* checked her facts carefully to ensure that her articles contained nothing (b) *slanderous.*

    a. _____
    b. _____

18. After several years of acquiescing in his crusade, the U.S. Senate (a) *censored* Senator McCarthy. He had (b) *flouted* legal and legislative procedures for years as he (c) *slandered* government employees with accusations of Communist party membership and Communist sympathies. After the Senate took official action, McCarthy's (d) *affectiveness* was ended.

    a. _____
    b. _____
    c. _____
    d. _____

19. Ernest Hemingway was admired for his (a) *sparse* prose style.

    a. _____

20. His neighbors considered him smug and (a) *complaisant.* He often bragged about his collection of paintings, which, while old, had been (b) *appraised* by experts and were deemed (c) *worthless.* Visitors to the house invariably felt pressured to (d) *complement* him on it.

    a. _____
    b. _____
    c. _____
    d. _____

21. The mathematician was (a) *honing* in on a proof of the 300-year old theorem that had (b) *eluded* many others over the centuries.

    a. _____
    b. _____

22. The longer she worked at the company, the more (a) *ambivalent* she felt about (b) *it's* direction.

    a. _____

    b. _____

23. The newspaper (a) *media* is becoming more and more sensationalistic in order to compete with television.

    a. _____

24. The (a) *émigré* parents took special pains to teach their American-born children about their (b) *forbears* in the old country.

    a. _____

    b. _____

25. The groom decided to (a) *forgo* his wedding reception to watch the basketball game. The bride loved him enough to (b) *forbear* in the face of this indignity, but over a period of time the marriage (c) *floundered* over the issue of his almost unbelievable sports fanaticism.

    a. _____

    b. _____

    c. _____

26. Experts agreed that the overall business (a) *strategy* was deeply flawed, but (b) *continual* adjustments in (c) *tactics* saved the company from disaster. (d) *Fortuitously* for management, however, interest rates (e) *fortunately* declined, compensating for severely (f) *averse* business conditions.

    a. _____

    b. _____

    c. _____

    d. _____

    e. _____

    f. _____

27. Long-term changes in the (a) *ecology* threaten to (b) *envelop* the earth in a layer of gases that will trap solar heat in the atmosphere and melt the polar ice caps.

    a. _____

    b. _____

28. Thelma and Louise refused to (a) *except* the consequences of their actions, and felt that they had no (b) *alternate* but to flee the law.

    a. _____

    b. _____

29. Her grades in history reflected the fact that she was nearly totally (a) *disinterested* in the subject.

    a. _____

30. The high school (a) *principal* made a (b) *precipitous* decision on how to discipline one of the students and ended up being sued.

    a. _____

    b. _____

31. The children never take my (a) *advise* (b) *accept* when their grades start to fail.

    a. _____

    b. _____

32. The city economy (a) *shrunk* during the recession and the entire city government was desperately (b) *straitened.* Budget cuts threatened to (c) *reek* havoc with municipal services.

    a. _____

    b. _____

    c. _____

33. The psychologist told her that her anxiety (a) *sprang* from a deep-seated fear of the unknown. She found his explanation (b) *specious* and said, "I pay you $90 for that kind of insight? Enough (c) *already.*"

    a. _____

    b. _____

    c. _____

ANSWERS

1. a. Correct b. corroborate

2. a. Honorable b. Correct c. prosecutor d. coherent e. Correct f. Correct g. mitigating

3. a. Correct b. sheared c. vise d. contemptuous

4. a. energized b. eminent c. Correct d. Correct e. evasion

5. a. irrespective b. well c. who's d. Correct

6. a. Correct b. elude c. Correct d. overlooking e. psychiatrist

7. a. ordnance b. destroyed c. corps d. Correct e. Correct f. fewer g. corpse

8. a. perquisites b. prerequisite c. principle d. simplistic e. worthless

9. a. criterion b. Correct

10. a. Correct b. silicone

11. a. discriminatory

12. a. officious   b. simple   c. Correct

13. a. silicon   b. Correct   c. strategy

14. a. distracted   b. oculist or ophthalmologist

15. a. Correct   b. Correct   c. Correct   d. sarcastic

16. a. nonflammable   b. prerequisite

17. a. always   b. libelous

18. a. censured   b. Correct   c. Correct   d. effectiveness

19. a. spare

20. a. complacent   b. Correct   c. Correct   d. compliment

21. a. homing   b. Correct

22. a. Correct   b. its

23. a. medium

24. a. Correct   b. forebears

25. a. Correct   b. Correct   c. foundered

26. a. Correct   b. Correct   c. Correct   d. fortunately   e. fortuitously   f. adverse

27. a. environment   b. Correct

28. a. accept   b. alternative

29. a. uninterested

30. a. Correct   b. precipitate

31. a. advice   b. except

32. a. shrank   b. Correct   c. wreak

33. a. Correct   b. Correct   c. Correct

Final Vocabulary Power Self-Test

In the blank at the left of each question, write the number of the definition that best fits the meaning of the word italicized. Most words were specifically covered in the book; some were not, but are made up of word parts studied. In either case, use your knowledge of word parts to help you choose the best answer, according to the literal meaning of the word. (If you plan to take this test before reading the book and again afterward, be sure to write your answers on a separate sheet of paper, not in the book.) Answers are given following the self-test.

1. Hank hit an *unprecedented* number of home runs.
   (a) without an earlier model or pattern
   (b) clear and uncomplicated
   (c) without reasoning or planning to

2. Mr. Ormsby is the chief *malefactor* in this story about nineteenth-century millionaires.
   (a) leader
   (b) mill owner
   (c) evildoer

3. The president said the pact with the European countries would be *conducive* to world peace.
   (a) opposed to
   (b) leading to
   (c) not relating to

4. The plastic surgeon was continually bogged down in expensive *litigation.*
   (a) remodeling
   (b) intensive medical care
   (c) lawsuits

5. John was unexpectedly overcome by a feeling of *claustrophobia.*
   (a) fear of water
   (b) fear of high places
   (c) fear of being shut in

6. A *malevolent* expression indicates:
   (a) good will
   (b) illness
   (c) evil intent

7. A *cursory* reading of a book is:
   (a) extremely careful
   (b) very pleasurable
   (c) a hasty running through

8. Tim is *credulous.*
   (a) too readily believing
   (b) dull or stupid
   (c) easygoing

9. Ms. Beamis is a *recluse.*
   (a) one who loves animals of all kinds
   (b) one who loves only money
   (c) one who shuts himself or herself away from society

10. To *recapitulate* a lecture is to:
    (a) make a summary
    (b) take something apart
    (c) change the original meaning

_____ 11. Government statistics showed a *per capita* expense of $4,000.
(a) by or for the government
(b) by or for each person
(c) an amount left after deductions

_____ 12. Our instructions were quite *explicit.*
(a) given by someone in authority
(b) clearly stated
(c) without detail

_____ 13. Ms. Hopkins called attention to Roger's *deferential* manner of treating her.
(a) showing dislike
(b) showing ignorance about something
(c) showing respect

_____ 14. To be accused of *duplicity* is to be accused of:
(a) spiteful actions
(b) double-dealing
(c) insincere efforts to please

_____ 15. The patient's behavior is *regressive.*
(a) going back to an earlier level
(b) moody and changeable
(c) lacking control

_____ 16. The equipment used in this kind of construction in very *ponderous.*
(a) heavy and unwieldy
(b) old-fashioned and unsuitable
(c) quite expensive

_____ 17. I was soon aware of an *incongruity* between his words and his actions.
(a) lack of agreement
(b) agreement
(c) missing connection

_____ 18. The reporter questioned the *efficacy* of such cold remedies.
(a) hidden danger
(b) side effect
(c) ability to carry out its intended function

19. The gift brought on a feeling of *elation.*
     (a) disappointment
     (b) reward for services rendered
     (c) joy or pride

20. By the time she was thirty-three, she was a *facile* writer.
     (a) able to write with ease
     (b) given to serious discussions
     (c) having great merit

21. The construction of the bridge was a *superlative* engineering accomplishment.
     (a) requiring the cooperation of many people
     (b) carried to the highest level
     (c) seeming to require divine or nonhuman help

22. The Smith children were *incorrigible* last Saturday evening.
     (a) not easily discouraged
     (b) having physical ills of some kind
     (c) unmanageable or uncontrollable

23. His anger was expressed in an *incontinent* flow of words.
     (a) not logical; emotional
     (b) not entirely clear and connected
     (c) not held back or controlled

24. Until she was eighteen she had never done any *introspective* thinking.
     (a) imaginary
     (b) unlimited
     (c) looking within

25. The *sentimentality* of the poem appealed to him.
     (a) exaggerated tender feeling
     (b) characteristics of old age
     (c) guilty feeling

26. A *sedentary* occupation:
     (a) involves a great deal of sitting
     (b) centers on an important area of work
     (c) supports a more important job

27. To have the *stamina* of a long-distance runner is to have:
    (a) a special body rhythm
    (b) expert physical coordination
    (c) endurance

28. If you have a *presentiment* of danger, you have:
    (a) foreknowledge
    (b) an unjustified opinion
    (c) a slight indication

29. *Diaphanous* material allows something to:
    (a) be seen through it
    (b) be attached to it
    (c) be attracted to it

30. What does an *astringent* lotion do?
    (a) It binds the skin tight.
    (b) It loosens the skin.
    (c) It makes a person look younger.

31. Sylvia refused to participate in any *occult* ceremonies.
    (a) mysterious; based on hidden knowledge
    (b) unprepared or unrehearsed
    (c) costly or time-consuming

32. At that time Venice was an *affluent* society.
    (a) living on or near water
    (b) shifting locations periodically
    (c) having an abundance of wealth for most members

33. To *abjure* dishonesty in politics is to:
    (a) swear oneself as being opposed to dishonesty in politics
    (b) swear to the existence of dishonesty in politics
    (c) be upset by dishonesty in politics

34. The first explorers were surprised to discover these natives worshipping *anthropomorphic* gods.
    (a) cruel to human beings
    (b) having both sexes in one being
    (c) having human characteristics

35. The author called Senator Hargis a clever *demagogue.*
     (a) public speaker
     (b) unimportant official
     (c) one who leads the people by appealing to their worst nature

36. An *autonomous* state is:
     (a) self-ruling
     (b) just coming into being politically
     (c) dominated by machines and industry

37. A *eulogy* is a speech in which someone is:
     (a) belittled
     (b) praised
     (c) welcomed

38. A great deal of publicity was given to his *eccentricities.*
     (a) illegitimate children
     (b) illegal actions
     (c) unconventional actions

39. In *retrospect* I see that my problems were really minor.
     (a) looking backward
     (b) seeing from all angles
     (c) admitting error

40. *Hyperactive* children are:
     (a) underactive
     (b) overactive
     (c) troublesome to deal with

41. The humor in the movie is based on *anachronisms.*
     (a) predictions about the future
     (b) incidents taken from the past
     (c) errors in time

42. A *panacea* for the world's ills is a:
     (a) forced action
     (b) one-sided solution
     (c) cure-all

43. A *heterogeneous* group of people contains people:
    (a) unable to reproduce
    (b) having similar characteristics
    (c) having different characteristics

44. How many people does it take to form a *sextet?*
    (a) two
    (b) six
    (c) seven

45. If something is two *millimeters* wide, it is:
    (a) two thousand meters wide
    (b) two-thousandths of a meter wide

46. Ms. Darnell *acceded* to our request.
    (a) yielded
    (b) denied
    (c) considered fully

47. The *diffusion* of his energies left him incapable of finishing all his projects on time.
    (a) decline
    (b) rapid use
    (c) being scattered over a large area

48. He referred to his mistress *euphemistically* as his "social secretary."
    (a) in a manner marked by the lack of any emotion
    (b) in a manner marked by emotional overtones
    (c) in a manner marked by using pleasant-sounding rather than harsh or realistic words

49. An *omnivorous* creature:
    (a) hunts only at night
    (b) eats both plant and animal substances
    (c) has no enemies more powerful than itself

50. In the fairy tale a witch is said to be fond of *metamorphosing* small children.
    (a) leading small children astray
    (b) making accidents happen to small children
    (c) changing the form of small children

ANSWERS

1. (a) without an earlier model or pattern ("without something having gone before")
2. (c) evildoer ("one who does evil or bad")
3. (b) leading to ("marked by leading together")
4. (c) lawsuits ("act of carrying on a lawsuit")
5. (c) fear of being shut in ("fear of closed places")
6. (c) evil intent ("marked by bad will")
7. (c) a hasty running through ("marked by running")
8. (a) too readily believing ("marked by believing")
9. (c) one who shuts himself or herself away from society ("one shut back")
10. (a) make a summary ("carry to a head again")
11. (b) by or for each person ("per head")
12. (b) clearly stated ("folded out"; unfolded)
13. (c) showing respect ("marked by carrying down" one's own importance)
14. (b) double-dealing ("state of two folds")
15. (a) going back to an earlier level ("marked by stepping backward")
16. (a) heavy and unwieldy ("characterized by weight")
17. (a) lack of agreement ("state of not coming together")
18. (c) ability to carry out its intended function ("quality of making out")
19. (c) joy or pride ("state of being carried outside" oneself)
20. (a) able to write with ease ("able to do or make")
21. (b) carried to the highest level ("characterized by being carried above")
22. (c) unmanageable or uncontrollable ("not able to be ruled, not able to be made straight")
23. (c) not held back or controlled ("marked by being not held together")
24. (c) looking within ("characterized by looking inside")
25. (a) exaggerated tender feeling ("state of feeling")
26. (a) involves a great deal of sitting ("characterized by sitting")
27. (c) endurance ("ability to stand"—that is, to keep on one's feet)
28. (a) foreknowledge ("a feeling beforehand")
29. (a) be seen through it ("characterized by being clear throughout")
30. (a) It binds the skin tight. ("that which binds toward")
31. (a) mysterious; based on hidden knowledge ("marked by being covered up"—that is, hidden)
32. (c) having an abundance of wealth for most members ("characterized by flowing toward")

33. (a) swear oneself as being opposed to dishonesty in politics ("to swear away")

34. (c) having human characteristics ("having the shape of man")

35. (c) one who leads the people by appealing to their worst nature ("people leader")

36. (a) self-ruling ("characterized by self-rule")

37. (b) praised ("good speech," "act of saying good things")

38. (c) unconventional actions ("acts that are off-center")

39. (a) looking backward ("backward look")

40. (b) overactive ("marked by being excessively active")

41. (c) errors in time ("things that are opposed in time"—that is, not of the same time order)

42. (c) cure-all ("that which cures everything")

43. (c) having different characteristics ("characterized by being of different kinds")

44. (b) six ("that which is composed of six" people)

45. (b) two-thousandths of a meter wide (*millimeter* = "a thousandth of a meter")

46. (a) yielded ("yielded to")

47. (c) being scattered over a large area ("act of pouring apart")

48. (c) in a manner marked by using pleasant-sounding rather than harsh or realistic words ("in a manner based on pleasant statements")

49. (b) eats both plant and animal substances ("characterized by eating everything")

50. (c) changing the form of small children ("current act of changing the form")

Appendix

The prefixes and roots used in this program.

PREFIXES	MEANING	EXAMPLES
Greek		
a, an	without	adamant, amoral, atheism
anti, ant	against	antagonist, antibiotic, antisocial
cata	down	cataclysmic, catalyst, catapult
dia	across, through, thoroughly	diagonal, diaphanous, diathermy
epi	on, upon	epidermis, epitaph, epitomize
ec	out, outside	eccentric, ecstasy, mastectomy
eu	good, pleasant	eugenics, euphony, euthanasia
hyper	over, excessive	hyperbole, hypercritical, hypersensitive
hypo	under, less than	hypoactive, hypodermic, hypothesis
para, par	alongside	parallel, paraphrase, parody
peri	around, near	perigee, periphery, periscope
syn, sym, syl, sys	together, with	syllable, symposium, syntax, system

PREFIXES	MEANING	EXAMPLES
Latin		
a	toward	ascribe
ab, abs	from, away	aberrant, abrade, abstinence
ad (af, ag, al, am, an, ar, as)	to, toward	adore, aggravate, allocate, attract, ascribe
ante	before	antedate, antediluvian, anteroom
circum	around	circumference, circumspect, circumvent
com, con, col, co	with, together	commingle, congruent, conjugal, cooperate
counter, contra, contro	against, opposite	contraband, controversy, countermand
de	down, away	decelerate, depose, descend
dis, dif, di	apart, not	diffident, digress, discomfiture
ex, ef, e	out	efface, eject, exempt
inter	between	intermittent, interregnum, interstate
intra, intro	within	intrastate, intravenous, introvert
ob, oc, of, op	against	obtuse, occult, offend, oppose
per	through, thoroughly	percolate, permeate, perspicacity
post	after	posterior, postlude, postnatal
pre	before	precocious, presentiment, preside
pro	forward, in front of, in favor of	procreate, prolix, propose
sub	under, below	subarctic, subjugate, subterranean
super	over	superannuated, superficial, superfluous
trans	across, through, beyond	transcend, transient, transitory

ROOTS	MEANING	EXAMPLES
Greek		
anthrop, anthropo	man, mankind	anthropoid, misanthrope, philanthropy
arch	first, ancient, chief	archaic, archeology, oligarchy
chron	time	chronic, chronology, synchronize
dem, demo	people	demagogue, demographer, epidemic
dox	belief, teaching, opinion	doxology, orthodox, paradoxically
dyna	power	dynamite, dynasty, thermodynamics
gam	marriage	bigamy, misogamist, polygamy

ROOTS	MEANING	EXAMPLES
Greek		
gen	birth, race, kind	congenital, genealogy, progenitor
hydr	water	hydraulic, hydrophyte, hydroponics
log, logy	speech, study of, collection of	astrology, dialog, zoology
mega, megalo	great	megalopolis, megaton, megavitamin
micro	small	microbe, microcosm, microorganism
morph	form	amorphous, metamorphosis, polymorphic
neo	new	neoclassical, neolithic, neophyte
nom	rule, law, systematized knowledge	agronomist, autonomous, metronome
onym	name	acronym, anonymously, pseudonym
pan	all	panacea, pandemonium, pantheon
path	feeling, suffering, disease	apathy, pathetic, psychopath
phil	love	Anglophile, philanderer, philter
pod, ped	foot	podiatrist, centipede, tripod
ped	child	pediatrician, pedagogue, pedagogy
poly	many	polyandry, Polynesia, polysyllabic
polit, polis	city, citizen	cosmopolitan, Indianapolis, politician
proto	first, fundamental	protocol, protoplasm, protozoa
pyr	fire	pyre, pyromania, pyrophobia
scop	see	horoscope, periscope, telescope
the	god	apotheosis, polytheism, theocracy
Latin		
act, ag, ig	do, drive, carry on, move	activate, agility, agitate
am, amat	love, loving	amateur, amiable, amorous
anim	spirit	animation, magnanimous, animosity
aqu	water	aqualung, aquatic, subaqueous
bel, bell	war	antebellum, bellicose, belligerent
bene	good	benefaction, benevolent, benign
capt(t), cept, cip, ceiv, ceit	seize, take	captivate, conceit, deceive, perception, recipient
capit	head	capitol, decapitate, per capita

ROOTS	MEANING	EXAMPLES
carn	flesh	carnage, carnivore, reincarnation
cede, ceed, cess	go, move, yield	accede, proceed, recession
cid, cis	cut, kill	fratricide, genocide, incision
clam, claim	cry, shout	clamor, disclaim, reclamation
cogn	know, be acquainted	cognizant, incognito, precognition
clud, clus, clois, claus	shut, close	claustrophobia, cloister, exclude, preclude
corp	body	corporeal, corpuscle, incorporate
cred	believe	credence, credulous, incredible
cur, cour	run	courier, cursory, incursion
dict	say, speak, tell	dictator, jurisdiction, valedictorian
doc, doct	teach	docile, doctrine, indoctrinate
duct, duc	lead	aqueduct, seduce, seductive
fac, fact, fect, fic, feat, feas, fy	do, make	facile, factory, feasible, magnify, perfectionist, proficient
fer, lat	bear, carry	conifer, differentiate, relate
fid	faith	confidant, fidelity, perfidious
flex, flect	bend, twist	flexible, genuflect, reflection
frag, fract	break	fractious, fragile, infraction
fus, fund, found	pour	effusive, foundry, refund
grad, gress	step, go	aggressive, degrade, digress
greg	flock	congregate, desegregation, gregarious, segregate
jac, ject	throw, hurl	conjecture, ejaculation, eject
luc	light	elucidate, lucid, translucent
mal	bad	malady, malevolent, malodorous
mit, miss	send	emission, remittance, transmit
omni	all	omnipotent, omniscient, omnivorous
pens, pend, pond	hang, weight	appendage, dispense, ponderous
plic, pli, ply	fold, bend	complication, implicit, pliant
rad	root	abrade, radical, eradicate
reg, rig, rect	rule, straight, right	incorrigible, rectify, regimen
scrib, script	write	ascribe, conscription, nondescript

ROOTS	MEANING	EXAMPLES
sed, sid, sess	sit	assiduous, sedentary, subsidiary
sent, sens	feel	dissent, sensuous, sentiment
sequ, secut	follow	inconsequential, persecute, sequel
solv, solut	free, loosen	absolution, resolve, solvent
son	sound	dissonance, resonance, unison
spec, spic	look	inspect, perspective, retrospect
spir	breathe	aspire, expire, spirometer
string, strict	bind tight	astringent, constrict, stringent
tang, ting, tact, tig	touch	contiguous, contingent, intact, tangible
tempor	time	contemporary, tempo, temporize
ten, tin, tain	hold	incontinence, tenacious, tenure
tend, tens, tent	stretch	contentious, distend, extensive
tenu	thin	attenuate, extenuate, tenuous
tort	twist	contortion, retort, tortuous
tract	draw, pull	distract, intractable, traction
ver	true	veracity, verisimilitude, verity
vid, vis	see, look	invidious, providence, supervise
voc, vocat, vok	call, calling	advocate, convocation, invoke, vocal

SUFFIXES	MEANING
acy	quality of
age	(verb ending)
al	that which, being, relating to, characterized by
ally	(adverb form of al) manner
ance	act of, that which
ant	that which, marked by, one who
ary	place of, one who
ate	(verb ending, as in accelerate)
ate	(adjective ending) marked by
ation	act of, state of
atic	marked by
ence	quality of, act of

SUFFIXES	MEANING
ent	one who, marked by, that which, being, characterized by being
iac	one who
ial	characterized by being
ian	characterized by being, one who
ic	relating to, being characterized by, marked by, being, science of
ics	operation of
ical	characterized by, relating to
ion	act of, state of, process
ire	that which
ism	theory, practice, belief, condition, property of
ist	one who
ity	quality of, ability to, state of, that which, those who
ium	act of, that which
ize	(verb ending)
ly	(adverb ending) in the manner of
ment	state of, that which, result of
oid	like, resembling
or	one who
ory	relating to, place, characterized by, based on, marked by
ous	based on, relating to, having the quality of, being, marked by, characterized by, characterized by being
(e)ry	act of
um	characterized by being, that which
ure	state of
us	that which
y	(forming noun) state of, condition of, quality of, capacity of, act of, result of, process, that which
y	(forming adjective) full of, having quality of

Index